Discipline, Democracy, and Diversity:
working with students with behaviour difficulties

Angus H Macfarlane

NZCER PRESS
Wellington 2007

NZCER PRESS
New Zealand Council for Educational Research
PO Box 3237
Wellington
New Zealand

© Angus H Macfarlane, 2007

ISBN 978-1-877398-26-1

All rights reserved

Cover image by Donn Ratana
Designed by Cluster Creative
Printed by PrintLink, Wellington

Distributed by NZCER Distribution Services
PO Box 3237
Wellington
New Zealand
www.nzcer.org.nz

Dedication

This book is a tribute to the memory of my sister, Ann Hineaupaki Smith.

Contents

Acknowledgements	7
Preface	9
PART ONE Legacies and developments	**13**
Inclusion, theoretical models, causation	
1 Including students with behaviour difficulties: perceptions, perspectives, possibilities	15
2 Theoretical models: a platform for understanding behaviour	25
3 Behaviours: influencing factors, definitions, types	35
PART TWO Traversing the behaviour continuum	**49**
Strategies for responding to varying levels of behaviour difficulties	
4 Landmark developments in classroom management: strategies for responding to mild to moderate behaviour difficulties	51
5 Students on track at Railway School: strategies for dealing with severe behaviour difficulties	71
PART THREE Listening to culture	**95**
International perspectives on culturally responsive teaching, and the Hikairo Rationale: a culturally responsive approach for working with Māori students and whānau	
6 Culturally responsive teaching: evidence from classic research studies in the United States and New Zealand	97
7 The Hikairo Rationale: a culturally responsive approach for working with students with behaviour difficulties - Huakina mai: opening doorways - Ihi: being assertive - I runga i te manaaki: growing a caring community - Rangatiratanga: motivating learners - Kōtahitanga: linking home and school - Awhinatia: moving toward restorative practice - Orangatanga: developing a nurturing environment	115
PART FOUR Synthesis	**167**
Unity of purpose as a basis for action	
8 Navigating the choppy sea	169
References	177
Glossary of Māori terms	191
Index	195

Acknowledgements

Korihi te manu
Tākiri mai te ata
Ka ao, ka ao, ka awatea
Tīhei mauri ora

The bird calls
The day begins
There is light
There is life

Those who have travelled down the road of writing of a book can attest that it is an intriguing journey, one that can consume yet enthuse the writer in many ways. Throughout this journey, encouragement and support were forthcoming from my academy, from tribal entities, and from friends, colleagues, and family members.

I am grateful to the School of Education of the University of Waikato for granting me twelve weeks' sabbatical leave. For a considerable portion of that time I was generously accommodated, as a writer in residence, by the New Zealand Council for Educational Research in Wellington. Thank you for that support. I also truly appreciated the backing of the Ngāti Whakaue Education Endowment Trust and the Ngāti Rangiwewehi Rūnanga.

This project was mentored by Bev Webber, processed to print by Carlene Grigg, and edited by Anne Else. I thank you sincerely. Thanks to my colleague, Donn Ratana, whose artwork appears on the cover of the book. Finally, an acknowledgement to my wife Sonja Bateman, whose ongoing support, positive encouragement, and willingness to offer excellent suggestions were invaluable.

Kia ora tātou
Angus H Macfarlane

Preface

Origins of the book

Convening courses for graduate and undergraduate students on student motivation and behaviour has been part of my role in the School of Education of the University of Waikato since 1997. In 2004, a course on this topic was offered as a summer school option for the first time. Each year since, course enrolments have exceeded capacity, and evaluations of the course by participating students have been extremely positive. However, this did not prevent me and a colleague, Dr Vivien Hendy, thinking hard about what we would like to do even better. Given that the course is particularly focused on preparing teachers and teacher trainees to work effectively with students who present with behaviour difficulties, we felt that the course text needed to provide sufficient background information and content for the participants to understand which methods and strategies have been judged to work best, and how these can be most effectively implemented. More discussions ensued, culminating in the decision to produce a book designed to prepare teachers for the task of managing and meeting the needs of students who present with behaviour challenges.

Focus of the book

There is little doubt that the profession of teaching is becoming increasingly more multifaceted and demanding. The need for teachers to have a greater appreciation and understanding of theory, as well as the competence to put this understanding into practice, must not be underestimated. The combination of research scholarship and on-the-job experience will clearly support teachers to be more skilful managers of students with challenging behaviours. This is by no means an easy task, as the issues involved are both complex and broad. The main focus of this book, therefore, is to illustrate the links between behavioural theory and competent teaching practice. Initially, it explores some of the literature and theory. It then reflects this knowledge by way of a range of practical skills that can be applied within the context of today's diverse classrooms.

Throughout the process of writing the book, the constant point of reference was its title: *Discipline, Democracy, and Diversity: Working with Students with Behaviour Difficulties.* "Discipline" is about teaching and modelling responsible individual and collective behaviours that will encourage students to become self-motivated and self-regulated learners. "Democracy" is about putting into practice skilful and respectful approaches for meeting the needs of students experiencing behaviour difficulties. "Diversity" is about creating an inclusive and safe environment; one that stimulates the development of knowledge, creativity, acceptance, and participation, and encourages the expression of feelings. Rather than being seen as a hindrance, diversity highlights the richness that can ensue for teachers' own practice, as well as for the class as a whole, when difference is valued.

Audience and purpose

This book is written for beginning and experienced teachers who are developing an interest in working effectively with students who present with behaviour challenges. It is also intended for resource teachers, special education advisers, school psychologists, and paraprofessionals. It aims to offer a useful range of approaches, responses, practices, and procedures that teachers and other professionals might consider and apply. A recurring message in the book is the need for teachers to create a strong foundation in the learning environment, in order to extend academic achievement and promote positive student behaviour. This foundation includes building relationships, being well organised, having empathy, growing a repertoire of strategies, and maintaining a passion for learning and teaching in all its forms.

Organisation of the book

Part One explores the historical background of education services for students with behaviour difficulties. It covers the evolution of the theoretical models that serve to rationalise a structured set of ideas, descriptions, and explanations about behaviour.

The two chapters in Part Two each cover different levels of challenging behaviour. Chapter 4 focuses on responding to mild to moderate behaviour difficulties. It outlines some of the landmark developments in classroom management and their respective propositions about discipline, from noted contributors such as Jacob Kounin, Colin Smith, and Robert Laslett; Kevin Wheldhall and Frank Merrett; and Fredric Jones. Chapter 5 offers strategies for dealing with more severe behaviour difficulties.

Part Three encourages teachers to understand the importance of listening to culture. It strongly emphasises the importance of the role that culture plays in people's lives, and the implications of that role for those involved in working with Māori students experiencing behaviour difficulties at school, and their whānau (families). Chapter 6 provides summaries of culturally responsive teaching from studies in the United States and New Zealand. Chapter 7 introduces the Hikairo Rationale, an approach to behaviour management drawing on values emanating from the Māori world, then expands on its seven elements. While all seven overlap and interweave, each is individually characterised by concepts and principles that can ultimately be applied, firmly and democratically, through culturally responsive teaching.

Part Four draws the strands of the book together. It stresses that while many trials and tribulations, as well as bounties and rewards, accompany the perplexing issues associated with understanding and responding to behaviour difficulties, those involved in the field of education should never give up. A choppy sea can be navigated safely. As educators, we cannot change the past for students with behaviour difficulties. However, through skilled discipline—resonating with democracy, and valuing diversity—we can make a difference.

PART ONE

LEGACIES AND DEVELOPMENTS

Inclusion, theoretical models, causation

1 **Including students with behaviour difficulties:** perceptions, perspectives, possibilities

2 **Theoretical models:** a platform for understanding behaviour

3 **Behaviours:** influencing factors, definitions, types

CHAPTER 1

Including students with behaviour difficulties:
perceptions, perspectives, possibilities

Introduction

Amongst the many issues confronting education systems around the world, perhaps none is more pervasive, persistent, or pressing than supporting students considered to be at risk of educational and societal failure. Many of these students experience behaviour difficulties. Unacceptable and disruptive behaviour in schools ranks as one of the most pressing concerns of the teaching profession.

This is far from being a new phenomenon. Similar concerns were being raised in New Zealand as far back as the 1860s, when disaffected and challenging children were referred to as "city arabs". A police commissioner at the time reported that there were children growing up in habits of vagrancy, and drew links between the number of children roaming the streets, and the incidence of juvenile crime (Mitchell & Mitchell, 1985).

Over a century later, in 1995, a front page story carried the headline, "Educators told that violence on the rise in New Zealand schools" (*Education Weekly*, 1995, p. 1). Many similar headlines have followed. In September 2006, for example, an article in a large daily newspaper reported on educators calling for the removal of violent students from secondary schools, and challenging the view that every student has a right to mainstream education (Trevett, 2006).

Two months later, the principal of one of New Zealand's largest secondary schools espoused that transience and instability in the home meant that some students had no chance to put down roots—and that the better option was to provide special education outside of school (*Hamilton This Week*, 2006). In February 2007, a metropolitan newspaper reported that the Minister of Education had set up a $4.5 million fund to help schools deal with disruptive behaviour (*The Dominion Post*, 2007).

Although the debate about how to best manage students who present with behaviour difficulties has been raging since systems of compulsory education began, evidence from many countries does support the contention that teaching is becoming increasingly challenging and more complex. The role of teachers has changed significantly in the last three decades. Expectations have intensified, with a heavy emphasis being placed on accountability, increased responsibility, and in particular more personal involvement in the process of educational reform, curriculum development, and overall school improvement (Fullan & Hargreaves, 1991). As demands upon teachers continue to increase and their work becomes more intense and challenging, it becomes essential for them to reflect not only on their practice, but also on the conditions and pressures they encounter.

Looking back

It would be difficult to understand today's context with regard to students with behaviour difficulties, and the services provided for them, if we were to assume that current issues emerge solely from the present. The good intentions of the past have not necessarily guaranteed sound judgement, nor achieved the required outcomes. In retrospect, particular past activities and practices can be identified as responsible for the stigmatisation, labelling, and alienation of many young people with behaviour difficulties.

Other texts, (for example, Andrews & Lupart, 1993; Kauffman & Smucker, 1995) provide comprehensive historical accounts of approaches to the education of students with behaviour difficulties. They make it clear that services for the whole range of students with special education and social needs, including those with behaviour difficulties, have evolved in six distinct phases: institutionalisation and relative isolation; segregation; categorisation; integration; mainstreaming; and inclusion. Table 1.1 gives a brief summary of these six phases, and adds a more recent emerging trend, circumspection, that argues for more deliberation over providing for students with behaviour difficulties.

Table 1.1 The evolution of provision for students with behaviour difficulties

ERA	PROVISION	MAIN FEATURES
1880s	Institutionalisation, relative isolation	The initial emphasis grew out of a social welfare concern for children who were often neglected or abandoned. These "human warehouses" became a dumping ground for students rejected by or removed from their families.
1900–1950	Segregation	Special schools and classes formed. More residential schools set up.
1950–1970s	Categorisation	Increased numbers and categories, particularly for high-incidence learners. Emphasis on testing and labelling. Health camps for primary school students and activity centres for secondary school students with behaviour difficulties.
1980s–1990s	Integration	A philosophical and attitudinal shift away from emphasis on special classes toward a concern for educating children in the least restrictive environment. Growing backlash against special classes.
1990s	Mainstreaming	Accommodation of students with special needs in a regular education setting.
1990s	Inclusion	Merger of special and regular education into a unified educational setting.
2007	Circumspection	Because of the increasing manifestation of behavioural disorders, the view that every child has a right to a mainstream education is challenged in some quarters.

Inclusion

The notion of inclusion has prevailed since the 1990s. According to Hoover and Patton (1997), this model, involving the merging of special and general education, evolved to become and remain the preferred option. Its primary goal is to create classroom environments which enable all students to be present, to participate, and to have opportunities to learn and work together (Stainback, Stainback, East, & Sapon-Sevin, 1994). In the formative years of inclusion, the primary focus was on students with very high needs (Fuchs & Fuchs, 1994). However, it has steadily expanded to include students with moderate needs.

The central contention of inclusion is that students with special needs are entitled to be educated, and that their education should take place in regular education settings. Inclusive education promotes the philosophy that academic learning, social competence, social skills, attitude change, and positive peer relations are all more effectively cultivated in regular, mainstream settings. Inclusive philosophy espouses several fundamental characteristics and beliefs that range from concern for individualised support to school-wide approaches and a sense of community involvement (Lipsky & Gartner, 1999).

Inclusion and behaviour difficulties

Perhaps the most widespread consequence associated with inclusion has been the placement and retention of students with behaviour difficulties in regular classroom settings. Given that alternative placement settings for these students are not as accessible as they once were, mainstream schooling is challenged to look for ways to respond to and manage manifestations of unacceptable student behaviours that can curb the progression of learning and achievement.

These manifestations vary in terms of intensity, severity, frequency, and duration. Some students present overtly with behaviours such as noncompliance, aggression, or dishonesty. According to Mitchell, Buist, Easter, Moltzen, Macfarlane, Quinn, and Timutimu (cited in Mitchell, 1999), they tend to overreact or externalise their feelings. Others manifest particular behaviours more covertly, or internalise their feelings. They may appear worried, solitary, timid, disinterested, distressed, withdrawn, anxious, or depressed. These students are often overlooked. Yet others may intermittently exhibit a combination of both externalised and internalised behaviours. Whatever form challenging behaviours take (they are described in more depth and detail in later chapters), it is clear that teachers urgently require the necessary resources to enable them to respond effectively. This involves not only providing schools with specialist personnel, but also enabling teachers to acquire a repertoire of strategies specifically designed to help them respond to these challenges.

Special education developments in New Zealand

In New Zealand, the Special Education 2000 (SE2000) policy, introduced in the mid 1990s, was permeated by the notion that schools should become more inclusive. Its main aim was "to achieve, over the next decade, a world class inclusive education system that provides learning opportunities of equal quality to all students" (Ministry of Education, 1996, p. 5).

Over the last two decades, in New Zealand as internationally, the overall drive toward inclusion has led to a move away from excluding students with behaviour difficulties from regular classrooms and schools. This move prompted the Government to introduce provisions designed to support schools in managing the gamut of behaviours that seem to persistently intrude on the professional practice of teaching. These provisions cover both moderate and severe behaviour difficulties.

The moderate behaviour initiative

As part of the SE2000 policy, two key initiatives were implemented for students with moderate behaviour difficulties: the Special Education Grant (SEG) and the Resource Teachers: Learning and Behaviour (RTLB) service. The SEG funding began in 1997. It is allocated according to a formula based on the number of students on the school roll, and the decile ranking of the school. (All New Zealand schools are ranked on a decile scale of 1 to 10. The ranking is a measure of socioeconomic position, with decile 1 being the lowest.) The RTLB service was established in 1999. Its role is to provide itinerant specialist support teachers to work with teachers and students, in order to improve the educational outcomes for students with moderate learning and behaviour difficulties. Over 760 RTLB work in 190 clusters of schools throughout New Zealand. Forty-five RTLB Māori provide support specifically to meet the needs of Māori students (Ministry of Education, 2005). Davies and Prangnell (1999) point out that the size of the clusters and the number of RTLB placed in each cluster varies according to schools' requirements, natural groupings, and geographic and socioeconomic factors. Decisions about how the service is provided are made by each cluster's management team. These two school-based resources serve between 4 percent and 6 percent of the student population.

The severe behaviour initiative

In 1998, the Ministry of Education announced its intention to implement, nationally, a Severe Behaviour Initiative. Now managed by Group Special Education (GSE), a division of the Ministry of Education, this initiative is designed to serve that 1 percent of the student population who exhibit the most extreme behaviour difficulties in the school and the classroom. The two key dimensions are geographically based behaviour specialists and Centres for Extra Support (CES). Behaviour specialists work in multidisciplinary teams; they include educational and clinical psychologists, and special education advisers who have experience in education settings, including early childhood facilities, primary schools, and secondary schools. They provide in-school support and are committed to responding quickly to critical situations, and assisting in the management of severely inappropriate behaviour. CES provide in-class and in-school support for short periods, and sometimes support for students off-site (Davies & Prangnell, 1999).

Challenging the old beliefs

The direction and subsequent success of inclusive special education delivery in New Zealand depends on the smooth and efficient transition from previously accepted to currently preferred practices (Moore, Anderson, Timperley, Glynn, Macfarlane, Brown, & Thomson, 1999). Putting inclusive principles into practice in the current education environment in turn depends on a major paradigm shift away from the traditional emphasis on exclusion and segregation (the functional limitations paradigm) to an emphasis on inclusion and participation (the ecological paradigm). The goal is a unified education system that views student diversity as a source of enrichment and challenge.

The process of "constructing inclusion" (Thomas & Loxley, 2001) requires educators to challenge previously held beliefs and assumptions about how and where students' learning needs are best able to be addressed (Fuchs & Fuchs, 1994; Kauffman, 1997; Moore et al., 1999). Progressing inclusion for students with behaviour difficulties requires that educators come to see students and their learning more holistically, allowing a conceptual framework to be established upon which equitable practices and processes may be delivered (Karagiannis, Stainback, & Stainback, 1996). The success of this progression is likely to rely to a large extent on teachers' confidence and competence: confidence in the effectiveness and robustness of the structures supporting the programme delivery and subsequent learning outcomes, and competence in terms of having the necessary skills, abilities, resources, and support to deliver these programmes within an inclusive setting (Dyson & Gains, 1993; Watson & Giorcelli, 1999), which is able to respond effectively to the needs of students experiencing behaviour difficulties (Conway, 1999). Andrews and Lupart (1993) maintain that schools' resources must be realigned so as to provide maximum support for teachers in their daily efforts to help students achieve to their full potential. One way of accomplishing this is to draw on the knowledge base that special education has developed separately over the past decades, and incorporate this knowledge into general education practice, collaborative consultation, and organisational restructuring.

Teachers' perceptions of inclusion

Constructing inclusion has often met with a high degree of resistance from many educators. This reflected the belief that traditional remediation programmes, including the withdrawal of problematic students, were the only effective solution. More significantly, however, it reflected high levels of fear and anxiety about how educators might cope with the perceived demands of including students with behaviour difficulties in their classrooms.

The fact is that the work of practising and promoting the effective inclusion of students with behaviour difficulties largely defaults to the classroom teacher (Cook, Tankersley, Cook, & Landrum, 2000; Forlin, 1997; Rietveld, 1999; Stanovich & Jordan, 1998; Thomas & Loxley, 2001). Hardman, Drew, and Egan (1999) propose that the attitudes of teachers are the most influential factors in determining the success of inclusive education for these students.

It is clear that teachers bring their own set of belief systems and attitudes to the classroom context in general, and to the concept of inclusion in particular. Stanovich and Jordan (1998) suggest that teachers' personal attitudes toward inclusion can be placed along a continuum. At one end is the attitude that learning and behaviour problems exist *within* the student. Teachers at this end of the continuum prefer to operate within the context of the functional limitations paradigm, with its emphasis on exclusion and segregation. At the other end is the attitude that learning and behaviour problems largely result from the interaction *between* the student and the environment. Teachers at this end prefer to operate within the ecological paradigm, with its emphasis on inclusion and participation (Brown, Thomson, Anderson, Moore, Walker, Glynn, Macfarlane, Medcalf, & Ysseldyke, 2000).

In order for inclusive education philosophies to work effectively in classrooms and schools, a positive shift along this continuum in teacher attitudes and belief systems is desirable. But for this to take place, there must initially be a willingness on their part to want to make inclusion work, to seek out alternatives, and to accept that they may need to modify their practice (Moore et al., 1999).

What influences teachers' attitudes to individual students? Cook et al. (2000) outline four kinds of response displayed by teachers towards specific students: *attachment, concern, indifference,* and *rejection*. Attachment students appear to be high achieving and hard working, and elicit more praise and less criticism from teachers. These students indirectly reward teachers with appropriate behaviour and academic achievement. In doing so, they neither demand nor receive a significant investment of teacher time and energy. Concern students, however, take up a great deal of teacher time and energy, due to concerns about their academic progress. For these students, monitoring, feedback, and expectations all tend to be delivered at high levels by willing teachers, who do not have to deal with inappropriate behaviours from these students. Students in the indifference category are generally quiet and unobtrusive, and also tend to avoid teachers. Student–teacher interactions are mainly brief and cursory for this group, in sharp contrast with those of the concern students. Rejection students are those most likely to be under close surveillance from the teacher. These students stand out because of their social, attitudinal, and behaviour difficulties. Teacher–student interactions are most often related to behaviour issues, and the resultant negativity of these interactions is compounded by the difficulties these students experience in the area of learning.

It is no surprise that rejection students test teacher tolerance (Gerber, cited in Cook et al., 2000). Given that students who present with behaviour difficulties most often fall into the rejection group, it is clear that there will continue to be many challenges for teachers in practising and promoting inclusion. Cook and his colleagues contend that teachers hold attitudes of rejection towards included students with behaviour difficulties at "significantly higher proportions" than would be expected by chance (p. 118). They put this down to the fact that such students fall outside the bounds of typical instructional tolerance, are relatively unresponsive to modal instruction, and are fundamentally viewed as a source of frustration and stress by their teachers. Reinke and Herman (2002) go a step further, saying that as a result of intolerance and frustration, many teachers may be indirectly prompted into participating in, and indeed colluding with, coercive interactions with "rejection" students. Such interactions serve only to further alienate and exclude many students in what are generally perceived as inclusive education settings (Wilton, 1997).

In a New Zealand study that focused on the support needs for teachers for the inclusion of students with disabilities (Prochnow, Kearney, & Carroll-Lind, 2000), approximately half of the 123 teachers in the study reported that they were not receiving the type and level of support that they required. Learning and behaviour challenges were by far the most common areas of concern identified in terms of support needed. Many teachers indicated that they felt particularly unprepared to be the primary source of support for students with such challenging needs. Milligan (2001) also expressed concern, in terms of the

SE2000 policy, with regard to adolescents with moderate to severe behaviour difficulties. She considered it important to provide a range of strategies to meet a continuum of need, stating, "It must be remembered that students become alienated from schools for a variety of reasons. A co-ordinated range of strategies needs to link SE2000 policy more closely to policy safeguards beyond the *triangle* [that is, the SE2000 triangle showing the components of the provisions] such as Alternative Education" (p. 332).

This points to two pivotal issues: first, the issue of including students with behaviour challenges in mainstream settings, specifically those who present with extreme aggression; and secondly, the notion of withdrawal, and whether this is in any way compatible with—or part of—an inclusive philosophy. McLeskey and Waldron (1998) concede that in numerous settings, there have been a significant number of students for whom an appropriate, full-time education setting may not be appropriate. They contend that for students with behaviours described as extreme, education within a general classroom setting does not necessarily meet their needs. Moreover, such a placement may seriously disrupt the learning of other students, and significantly contribute to the stress levels and feelings of failure of the teacher.

While McLeskey and Waldron declare that some students may need to be removed temporarily from the mainstream into contexts specifically constructed to support them, they also express some concerns about this scenario. Their main concern is that when such students are regularly placed amongst others with similar labels and histories, they are therefore exposed to role modelling or contexts that serve only to reinforce or exacerbate issues of concern, ultimately marginalising these students as individuals even further. In some instances, such short-term withdrawals may benefit all parties, providing some degree of space for cooling off or respite. Still, other students may benefit from longer term education in an alternative programme. How long such an option should last, however, is obviously reliant on and informed by compassion, as well as the knowledge and skills of the teacher(s). The success of this option depends on the programme being targeted, adroitly operated, and well led by committed and qualified staff (see Macfarlane, 1995). Perhaps there is a core group of students for whom the regular classroom may not be the right option. The educational and social benefits that accrue for students in inclusive placements are well documented, but the debate surrounding the paradoxes of inclusion will continue.

Summary

There is little doubt that there was an initial level of resistance from schools and communities when the inclusive philosophy first surfaced in New Zealand schools, but progress has been sound over the last 15 years. The growth in stature of inclusive education has in part been fuelled by a gradual shift in societal values towards greater equity for all. This process has also been assisted by a greater understanding of learning processes, more informed attitudes toward and tolerance of difference, and the ongoing support (for students with learning and behaviour difficulties) provided by special educators and support services.

Teacher attitudes toward inclusion, and indeed toward included students who have behaviour difficulties, are undeniably one of the major factors impacting on the day-to-day success, or otherwise, of effective practice in classrooms and schools. For inclusion to operate fully within the classroom, it is imperative that teachers continue to challenge any previously held deficit-grounded belief systems, and embrace a more interventionist and ecological philosophy (Conway, 1999). Teachers' attitudes and perceptions need to model and reflect the true intent of inclusion, so that the students in their care are not only physically present in the classroom, but are also participating fully in the classroom community.

However, it is impossible to make uniformity in attitudes and belief systems mandatory, or even to see this as achievable, in this complex and challenging domain. It is essential that teachers are supported, listened to, and understood; and that they are not only exposed to ongoing professional development and training in the education of students with behaviour difficulties, but are also supported by the necessary resources, time, and professional expertise. It is not unreasonable to expect that the mechanisms and education professionals supporting teachers and classrooms go the extra mile in order to empower teachers who require more assistance and guidance. Going that extra mile, however, may not necessarily quell the ongoing conversations and debates about the pros and cons of inclusion—particularly when it relates to the issue of including students who present with behaviours at the severe end of the spectrum. Resources that support teachers in the areas of teaching, learning, and classroom management are absolutely essential.

CHAPTER 2

Theoretical models:
a platform for understanding behaviour

Introduction

What makes us behave as we do toward self, others, and the environment? How can we change our behaviour and the behaviour of others from inappropriate to appropriate, and from unacceptable to acceptable? As Walker and Shea (1999) point out, theories help us to respond to those questions. They can provide a useful guide for teaching practice, as well as for the type of assessment and intervention that is required in terms of challenging behaviours.

There is an old axiom that states: "There is nothing more practical than a good theory." Yet the chasm between theory and practice is one of the issues frequently raised within both preservice and inservice teacher training. It seems that many teachers would prefer just to get on with the job in hand, allocating little time or thought to theory. Porter (1996) contends that teachers who hold this position may unknowingly perpetuate unsuccessful practices. She adds that this occurs not because of incompetence, but because the underlying ideas (the theories) that are driving the teachers' responses are not helping.

Theories serve to rationalise and make visible a structured set of ideas and practices. The more organised one's ideas, the more effective one can be in responding to challenging behaviour in the classroom. Theorising about learning and behaviour, therefore, can provide what Porter refers to as:

... an orderly set of beliefs, concepts and models that is used to describe, explain and predict behaviour ... If we simply rely upon what works we will have no system for understanding what to do and when. We may continue to respond to new situations with past models when new strategies are needed. (1996, p. 7)

Leading researchers in the field (Ashman & Elkins, 1998; Bishop & Berryman, 2006; Fraser, Moltzen, & Ryba, 2005; Hallahan & Kauffman, 1988; Kauffman, 1997; Peterson & Ishii-Jordan, 1994; Wearmouth, Glynn, & Berryman, 2005; Wheldall & Merrett, 1989) contend that theorising about learning and behavioural difficulties requires asking many questions in order to better understand the way people behave. Finding the answers to such questions, according to Kauffman (1997), is an intricate and complex task.

A useful theory is one that provides focus and direction without blinding us to other issues. Such theories generate a range of ethical and educationally valid solutions to educational problems. But theories come in different shapes and forms, and often serve different educational purposes. They propose different approaches to learning and behaviour, and will often determine the particular range of strategies that can and should be considered in particular instructional environments. Some theories have a greater orientation toward learning, others toward behaviour. However, there is also considerable conceptual overlap among them.

Walker and Shea (1999) identify and expand on four theoretical positions which they refer to as "models of human behaviour": psychodynamic, biophysical, behavioural, and environmental. This chapter looks at the first three, and also at two additional models: ecological and sociocultural. It goes on to consider the implications of each for classroom guidelines. Teachers need to think about whether the model in question describes the behaviour that they regularly encounter, and if it fits with their area of influence.

There is a vast range of explanatory models of human behaviour and the five introduced here are by no means exhaustive. The intention is to offer an overview of how behaviour is understood from five different theoretical perspectives, rather than a comprehensive review, such as those provided by Kauffman (1997), Charles (2002), and Walker and Shea (1999).

The psychodynamic model

Psychodynamic theorists perceive the causes of human behaviour as residing within the individual. The many forms of psychodynamic theories suggest that undesirable behaviour is the result of some form of inner turmoil or tension among the dynamic parts of one's personality. Brigham and Brigham (2005) contend that acceptable behaviour will be impossible until these tensions are resolved through a psychotherapy-oriented approach.

Behaviour management interventions derived from the psychodynamic model may be useful when it is assumed that in the case of emotional and behavioural disorders, the focus should be not on the behaviour itself, but on a pathological imbalance among the dynamic parts of one's personality, leading to unconscious conflicts. As a result, these students may be ignored by some peers, overly rejected by others, and used as scapegoats by a few. Being ignored, rejected, or made to feel embarrassed can in turn lead to behaviour that will affect further facets of the student's functioning, including academic achievement (Walker & Shea, 1999).

Brigham and Brigham (2005) explain that the implication for educators working within a psychodynamic model is to provide a permissive and accepting classroom environment, so that the student is able to work through his or her emotional conflicts. Counselling and other forms of talking interventions are often associated with this model of understanding behaviour. Within this model, it is suggested that students learn through a process of subconscious identification with significant adults in their lives. This means that the student's perspectives about the teacher's personal appearance, attitudes, and behaviour are important factors in teaching which must be evaluated continuously. According to Jones (1992), research and theory in classroom management and therapeutic interventions support a de-emphasis on control procedures, such as positive reinforcement and shaping. Working within this psychodynamic model calls for the incorporation of insight-oriented interventions into school-based programmes for learners with behaviour issues. Some of these include counselling techniques, life-space interviewing, and reality-therapy interviewing. The expressive media are a way of indirect behaviour-management intervention, and social-skills curricula may be applied to instruct students in prosocial behaviours.

In this model, the classroom emphasis is placed on developing a psychologically healthy atmosphere, accepting the young person and the pathological condition without reservation, and encouraging and assisting the student in learning. In order to promote and enhance the student's learning, the teacher must pitch learning activities at a level, and under circumstances, which enable him or her to experience success. The role of educational therapist is not one that is readily sought by teachers, and can be seen as time consuming and unproductive. Nevertheless, educators should not underestimate the power of talking with their students, and involving counsellors and other qualified professionals to help students make decisions about their behaviour.

The biophysical model

The biophysical model emphasises the organic origins of human behaviour. It postulates a relationship between physical defects, malfunctions and illnesses, and the individual's behaviour (Walker & Shea, 1999). Two primary subgroups of this model are the deficit and developmental theories (discussed by Shroeder and Shroeder, cited in Walker & Shea, 1999). The deficit subgroup sees the causes of behaviour disorders as related to genetics, temperament, nutrition, and neurological dysfunction. The developmental subgroup sees the causes as including neurological organisation, perceptual motor learning, psychological readiness, sensory integration, and development. Costello (cited in Walker & Shea, 1999) contends that:

> There are approximately 4000 disorders known to be caused by genetic defects. Among the most commonly known are Down syndrome, sickle cell disease, cystic fibrosis, and haemophilia. Because genetic disorders are permanent, chronic, and complex, they tend to evoke labelling. As a consequence, they impact on the lifestyle of the individual and the family. (p. 288)

Not surprisingly, intricate intervention processes are often indicated for the behaviours explained in this model. Brigham and Brigham (2005) assert that educators need to be aware of biophysical explanations, because they will see a number of students whose behaviour is related to a genetic or chemical condition. Though not the dominant theory of causation in the education of young people, the biophysical model does have proponents among professionals and parents of children with profound emotional and behavioural disorders. For example, schizophrenia, autism, depression, hyperactivity, and selective mutism are all able to be associated with organic origins. Some forms of problem behaviour, such as those just mentioned, respond better to medical treatment than to other forms of intervention (Brigham & Cole, 1998). Brigham and Brigham (2005) however, point out that educators are not trained in a biophysical discipline, and should be cautious before offering a biophysical explanation for a given behaviour.

Walker and Shea (1999) note that several curative and preventative medical interventions have been developed to mitigate or modify the effects of biological defects. These include prenatal and postnatal health care, appropriate nutrition and diet, and genetic counselling. The teacher plays an important role in ensuring that students receive medication, and most schools have very clearly outlined guidelines for planning how the medication will be administered and by whom, as well as for establishing direct communication among all concerned parties. Certain protocols apply; for example, it is essential to ensure that the decision to use medication is made appropriately. The teacher should never initiate a child's direct referral to a physician, and should not attempt to coerce parents to pursue or accept any particular medical treatment. However, it is fitting for teachers to inform parents about any difficulties with which children present.

Often schools and state educational agencies (such as health camps) provide support personnel for teachers of students with these types of biological issues. Teachers should not have to go it alone when working with such students. Behaviour therapists, psychologists, physical therapists, and nurses are all available to provide valuable services and guidance. The teacher has a pivotal role of support for these other professionals, including referral, collaboration, dispensation and safeguarding of medication, and modification of classroom structure and curriculum content. Often, the teacher who is influenced by the biophysical model will emphasise order and routine, frequent repetition of learning tasks, sequential presentation, and the reduction in extraneous environmental stimuli (Walker & Shea, 1999).

Monitoring of medication and participating as a member of a disciplinary team are important roles for teachers. Most importantly, they should display empathy and understanding with these young people.

The behavioural model

The behavioural model, including behaviour modification techniques and other applications to behaviour issues, has its roots in the writings of Bandura (1977) and Skinner (1971), among others. Walker and Shea (1999) propose that while the traditional debates have lingered on in terms of the various constructs and interventions within this model, practitioners have successfully applied its principles to a variety of human situations.

The behavioural explanation suggests that all behaviour is learnt as functions of events within the environment. Brigham and Brigham (2005) add to this explanation as follows:

> When maladaptive behaviours are observed, they should be considered to be the outcomes of inappropriate learning. Similarly, adaptive behaviours are the result of learning appropriate responses to various prompts in the environment. Behavioural practitioners support or change behaviour by arranging antecedent events and consequences. A great deal of effort goes into making precise definitions of the behaviour in question and collecting objective reliable data regarding frequency, duration, setting, antecedent events, and the consequences surrounding the behaviour. (p. 2)

"Behaviour modification" refers to the overall process of shaping student behaviour intentionally through reinforcing those behaviours that are appropriate, and ignoring those that are not. According to Wearmouth et al. (2005), the field of applied behaviour analysis employs strategies based on behavioural principles, such as positive reinforcement, negative reinforcement, token economy, extinction, generalisation, and discrimination. Roberts (cited in Walker & Shea, 1999) sums up the principles of reinforcement as follows:

1. Reinforcement always follows the exhibition of the behaviour.
2. The behaviour should be reinforced as soon as possible after it occurs.
3. The reinforcement must be appropriate for the individual or group being reinforced. A reinforcer is effective only if the individual or group being reinforced perceives the reinforcer as rewarding or punishing.
4. Many small rewards, presented frequently, are more effective than a few big ones. (p. 46)

Shaping is a procedure that exemplifies a small-steps strategy and is based on training and reinforcing each step (or behaviour) in a planned sequence until a final goal is achieved. According to Cole and Chan (1990) shaping usually works best when the teacher or aide is positioned to provide one-to-one tutoring and monitoring. When it is determined that the accepted behaviour is acquired, the intervention strategy or stimulus is gradually removed; that is, fading occurs.

Many educators are concerned that this approach is perhaps too clinical and robotic, with a tendency toward excessive teacher control. However, over a reasonably lengthy span of time it has been proved that each of the chief principles of this model—reinforcement, shaping, and fading—can be applied effectively in learning environments.

The ecological model

The ecological or integrative framework stresses that the understanding of human development and behaviour requires examination of the contexts of interactions in several settings (Bronfenbrenner, 1979). The home and the school are the critical environments in a child's world; they usually include the classroom, peer group, and family. Proponents of this approach insist that rather than focusing exclusively or primarily on the behaviour of the target student, ecological practitioners need to assess environment–behaviour interactions, as well as the ecological contexts in which student behaviours occur.

In order to be effective, educators and parents need to focus their primary efforts on the microsystem of school and home. According to Ysseldyke and Christensen (1998), the child's instructional needs in relation to the classroom context, and in relation to the home as a source of support for classroom learning, should be of primary concern when designing interventions. This is because educators have more direct control over the influences that occur at this microsystem level.

In a quantitative synthesis of about 3,000 studies in which causal influences on students' affective, behaviour, and cognitive outcomes were analysed, Walberg (cited in Ysseldyke & Christensen, 1998) located three major causal influences on student learning. The first was aptitude, which took into account ability, development, and motivation. The second was instruction, which considered the amount of student engagement and the quality of the instructional experience. The third was environment, where the emphasis of home, peers, classroom climate, and television were primary contributors. Given the bearing that these three influences can have on student behaviour, it appears that the interventions applicable within the ecological model would centre on many of the sound principles of classroom management. At the classroom level, the prominent factors include lesson organisation, lesson presentation, lesson momentum, student engagement, student accountability, and the mix of joy and challenge. At the home–school level, each would have to uphold affirming views of diverse cultural backgrounds, and each would need to listen to and respect the integrity and status of the other.

The ecological approach, according to Brigham and Brigham (2005), has the benefit of being less intrusive, because it employs naturally occurring supports already existing in the environment. These supports need to be built on. The expansion of teachers' skills must also be a key imperative.

The sociocultural model

Current conceptualisations of sociocultural theory draw heavily on the work of Vygotsky (1978), as well as later theoreticians (see, for example, Bruner, 1996). A key feature of this emergent model of human development is that higher order functions develop out of social interaction. Vygotsky argues that a child's development cannot be understood by a study of the individual. We must also examine the social world in which that individual has developed. A depiction of this social world is presented by a noted Māori scholar, Makereti (also known as Maggie Papakura). She describes the social ecology for Māori as the child being absorbed in the whānau, just as the whānau is absorbed in the hapū, and the hapū in the iwi (see Penniman, 1986).

Barbara Rogoff (2003) begins her text on the cultural nature of human development by stating that as a biological species, humans are defined in terms of their cultural participation. This is compatible with Phinney and Rotheram's (1987) contention that there are ethnically linked ways of thinking, feeling, and acting that are acquired through socialisation. Socialisation is taken to mean the way that youngsters are raised, along with the cultural tools that are both inherited and transformed by successive generations. Rogoff offers the following explanation:

> Vygotsky argued that children learn to use the tools for thinking provided by culture through their interactions with more skilled partners in the *zone of proximal development*. Through engaging with others in complex thinking that makes use of cultural tools of thought, children become able to carry out such thinking independently, transforming the cultural tools of thought to their own purposes. Interactions in the zone of proximal development allow children to participate in activities that would be impossible for them alone, using cultural tools that themselves must be adapted to the specific activity at hand. (pp. 50–51)

Assuming that the cultural context in which a child is reared shapes his or her thinking and provides tools for organising meaning and shaping behaviour, then this view (the sociocultural perspective) has profound implications for teaching and schooling. For a start, the zone of proximal development is a region of activities that individuals can navigate with the help of more capable peers or adults. Secondly, this zone can be composed of different levels of expertise of individuals (students and teachers), and it can include artefacts such as books, computers, and other information technology materials. Thirdly, this approach promotes the notion that students working in groups can master learning better than students working alone (see Slavin, 1990).

One proposal that would seem to emerge from this model is that which advances a vision of the culturally responsive teacher. Villegas and Lucas (2002) view culturally responsive teachers as those who:

- have sociocultural consciousness; that is, those who recognize that the ways people perceive the world, interact with one another, and approach learning, among other things, are deeply influenced by such factors as race/ethnicity, social class, and language. This understanding enables teachers to cross the cultural boundaries that separate them from their students.
- have affirming views of students from diverse backgrounds, seeing resources for learning in all students rather than viewing differences as problems to be solved.
- have a sense that they are both responsible for and capable of bringing about educational change that will make schooling more responsive to students from diverse backgrounds.
- embrace constructivist views of teaching and learning. That is, they see learning as an active process by which learners give meaning to new information, ideas, principles, and other stimuli; and they see teaching largely as a process of inducing change in students' knowledge and belief systems.
- are familiar with their students' prior knowledge and beliefs, derived from both personal and cultural experiences.
- design instruction that builds on what students already know while stretching them beyond the familiar. (p. xiv)

Clearly, the sociocultural model of behaviour encompasses much more than this brief summary. But the perspectives offered are important points to consider when examining the communicative, cognitive, and behaviour tendencies of learners—and of teachers.

Summary

This chapter provides a conceptual schema or framework for the analysis of methods and strategies for behaviour management, and how they can be better understood in the context of their origin. Emanating from these models are the ideas and beliefs that guide educators' actions with young people. What we believe about the behaviour of students affects how we respond and act toward them.

Teachers control their own perceptions and actions about students' learning and behaviour. In today's classrooms, theoretical models relating to behaviour difficulties are a starting point toward gaining a better understanding of the factors that cause such difficulties, and the different forms of behaviours that exist in schools and society.

Kauffman (1997) stresses that there is not only one way of knowing. However, he does believe that some ways of knowing are better than others for certain purposes. The most useful scientific information for teachers, he believes, "is that which is derived from controlled experiments that reveal how the social environment can be arranged to modify behavior and how individuals can be taught self-control" (p. 123).

This reinforces the importance of evidence-based practice in finding the links between differing teaching approaches and the learning and behaviour of students. Synthesising best evidence, along with the messages rooted in the theoretical models, confirms the enormous power that teachers have over the social environment of the classroom.

CHAPTER 3

Behaviours:
influencing factors, definitions, types

Introduction

What are the factors that influence behaviour? How are behaviour disorders defined? What are the various types of behaviour difficulties occurring in schools, and, technically, how are they described? If you spend some time among teachers, you will quickly encounter a wide range of viewpoints about the sources of behaviour difficulties, and an equally wide range of descriptions for the behaviours occurring in schools. Fraser and Moltzen (cited in Fraser, Moltzen, & Ryba, 2000) suggest that while many people have constructed their own personal theories about the causes and types of learning or behaviour difficulties, it is important to understand the explanations if we are committed to creating opportunities for these students to experience success. This chapter will provide some understanding of current explanations with regard to three main themes: causal factors, definitions, and types of behaviour.

Influencing environments

When we observe or read about people's behaviour difficulties, we wonder why they act the way they do. We search for explanations that will help us to understand what has gone wrong, and what—or even who—was to blame. We believe that understanding these things will help the process of putting matters right, and perhaps preventing future occurrences.

With these points in mind, four significant zones of environmental influences encompassing factors that may contribute to the development of behaviour difficulties—family, school, culture, and peers—are discussed here.

Family influence

The family and whānau (extended family) environment is of immense importance, given that this is the principal source of nurturance and the primary influence on the socialisation of the young. Winzer and Mazurek (1998) refer to the family structure as the mechanism that establishes norms of behaviour and teaches, explicitly and implicitly, social, moral, and psychological lessons to the developing child.

In New Zealand, a longitudinal research study of Dunedin children (Silva & Stanton, 1996) concluded that the majority of behaviour problems that are seen in the school years have their origins in very early childhood, probably within the first three years. The report of the Education and Science Committee Inquiry into Children in Education at Risk Through Truancy and Behavioural Problems (1995) has also proposed that many of the causes of behaviour difficulties stem from one's early years and from the nature of the home and family environment. The report outlined the vital role of early childhood in early intervention and in the prevention of later social and educational difficulties. There are a number of factors that impact on this situation. Family struggles, conflicts, and breakdowns, along with abuse, neglect, violence, and poverty, are perceived by many as being profoundly influential factors on the behaviour of young people. Poverty has been clearly associated with lower academic achievement and higher rates of behaviour problems. The impact of ongoing parental discord and divorce can be associated with young people experiencing depression, health problems, aggressive outbursts, and difficulty with learning. Emotional conflict and abuse can cause young people to withdraw, become aggressive, develop low self-esteem, and experience poor peer relationships (Smith, Polloway, Patton, & Dowdy, 2004).

The profundity of the influence that family circumstances have on a young person's development often erroneously frames the family as the chief culprit when students are in trouble for behaviour difficulties at school. Fraser (2004) contends that the family has become a popular scapegoat for many of society's ills, and considers that this is an unfair assumption to make. Indeed, schools cannot and must not use the concept of family factors being to blame for behavioural difficulties as an excuse for abdicating responsibility for the creation of a learning environment in which all students are accepted, and where programmes are provided which best meet their individual needs. Although many challenges originate at home, schools are duty bound to devise teaching and learning strategies that will help those students to achieve better outcomes at school. This may require changes in the ethos and philosophy both of schools and of teacher interactions with their students and their families.

Families face any number of risks that impact on their ability or capacity to raise their children successfully. Not all families are able to provide an adequate level of health and safety for all their members. Durie (2003) identifies three kinds of at-risk families. In unsafe families, some members show a fundamental lack of respect for others, which may erupt in violence. *Laissez-faire* families tend to be disorganised and lack any sense of direction or guidance. Restricted families are well intentioned, but lack the resources to convert aspirations into realities, and are often denied the benefits of society.

Durie (2003) goes on to identify several important capacities with the power to improve the status of families in modern times: caring and sharing; guardianship of cultural heritage such as language and physical icons; empowerment, such as entry into the marae, local communities, sport, and school; and planning ahead, for carrying out tasks such as balancing finances and managing the provision of children's education.

This cluster of capacities is important in helping to provide families with the ability to cope with contemporary problems. They should be seen not as a prescriptive list, but rather as a set of useful options to draw from and consider. It is argued that in fostering and drawing on these capacities, effective relationships between home and school will develop. The benefits for younger members of the family are likely to include improved school attendance, positive morale in the classroom, and the manifestation of appropriate behaviour across a range of contexts.

School influence

After the family, school is probably the most important socialising influence on children and young people. Kauffman (1997) sees school as the occupation of children and young people in our society, and success at school as therefore tantamount to success or failure as a person. Axelson (1993) contends that the educational system is in many ways a microcosmic replay of the larger society, with its economic problems, social conflicts, current fads, and intercultural events. Unsettling, emotional, or dramatic circumstances in the society will also influence students' feelings in the school environment. The immediate reality for school-age youth, however, is that their future, as well as their present, is most anchored and defined in their school experiences, which occupy a major portion of their lives. In a well known study of twelve London secondary schools, Rutter, Maugham, Mortimor, and Ouston (1979) pointed to the impact that schools and teachers have on the progress of young people in their care. They explained that for almost 12 years, during a formative period of their growth, youngsters spend almost as much of their waking life at school as at home, amounting to some 15,000 hours (hence the title of their book). Rutter and his colleagues are emphatic that schools are a central, "make it or break it" environment for many individuals.

Because the school environment is the one zone of behavioural influence over which teachers and principals have direct control, educators need to carefully and regularly evaluate the role of school and its relationship to the behaviour difficulties that many students experience:

> On each day of the school year, students have opportunities to learn and practice important academic skills and social behaviors, see and interact with peers and adults who model and promote prosocial skills, and receive recognition and constructive feedback about their behavior. When teacher-student interactions are generally positive, adult-directed, predictable, and engaging, schools can serve an important primary or universal prevention role in inhibiting the development of antisocial behaviors, promoting prosocial behaviors, and maximizing academic achievement. (Sugai, 2003, p. 530)

Schools may be able to ameliorate a student's behaviour problems, or make them worse. Kauffman (1997) notes that because many youngsters do not exhibit emotional or behaviour difficulties until they enter school, then educators should consider the possibility that the school experience may indeed ignite or precipitate such difficulties. In other words, it can be the cause as well as the cure. Conversely, while we might see the school system as being, in many ways, a microcosm of the larger society, the positive effects of a student's school experience (particularly if a youngster's home experiences are marred) can ripple outward like rays of hope.

Culture influence

Culture is dynamic and ever changing. Our culture determines what we eat and how we dress, our religious beliefs, and how and with whom we form and conduct our relationships. Culture is about our fundamental values—what matters. Culture is something which is lived. Mead (1997) refers to the notion of "what culture is not". It is not about outward forms of expression only, or something that other people have. It is not something that should or can be set aside or left at home when children go to school, so that they can get on with the "real" business of schooling. Young people do not shed their cultural nuances at the school gate; they take them with them into the classrooms and the playgrounds. This succinct definition of culture by Gay (2000) encapsulates its social and educational aspects:

> ... a dynamic system of social values, cognitive codes, behavioral standards, worldviews, and beliefs used to give order and meaning to our own lives as well as the lives of others. ... Culture determines how we think, believe, and behave ... and how we teach and learn. (pp. 8–9)

McInerney and McInerney (1998) argue that for education to be meaningful, it must take note of the learner's cultural background. In some cases, they say, the mismatch between teachers' understandings and children's backgrounds and culture can be so broad as to impede effective schooling. The need for educators to become good intercultural communicators certainly must be underscored at all levels of the profession, because:

> There will be communication problems for school personnel and learning problems for students when cultural differences are viewed only as deficiencies, when language differences are viewed only as deficits, when presumptions of intellectual inferiority are based on cultural group identity or membership, when individual potential goes unrecognized, when individual personality traits are distorted or over generalized according to cultural group identity or membership, and when negative self-concept is simplistically related to feelings of success and failure. (Axelson, 1993, p. 223)

Given the saliency of culture in everyone's life, attitudes held about the efficacy of teaching, or a teacher's ability to help students with behaviour difficulties, should be filtered through a cultural lens. This is not to imply an intention to elevate one worldview over another but simply to signal that differences exist in ideology and philosophy. According to Robinson and Howard-Hamilton (2000, p. 29): "understanding students' cultural values requires information about their group, exposure to a variety of experiences within the group, and an understanding of the sociopolitical dynamics of justice, oppression, history, and self-awareness." Educators need to be cognisant of the fact that not all individuals within a given culture will subscribe to what are generally perceived to be the dominant or core values of that culture. The studies of Judith Simon (1993) and Alison Jones (1989) show that while some teachers may have a deep concern for their indigenous minority cultures, that concern does not always transfer to emancipatory goals, but may be directed at fitting the students into their "places" within the existing setting. Expecting students from indigenous minority cultures to speak up and ask questions may well generate tensions and conflicts as they pertain to the concepts of whakamā (humility) and mana (respect for the status of the teacher). While the striving for cultural conscientiousness and hard work of many in the teaching profession must be recognised, there remains a prevailing and deep ignorance of Māori and minority cultures' values. Bishop and Glynn (1999) suggest that an expanded view of educational practices that address cultural diversity lies in the sense-making and knowledge-generating processes of these minority and indigenous cultures that the mainstream education system has effectively marginalised.

As Peterson and Ishii-Jordan (1994) point out, when looking at students' behaviour difficulties and the impact of cultural diversity, there are often more questions than answers. Some questions that need to be addressed include: What specific cultures are represented within the population of students identified as having behaviour difficulties? Are identification and interventions fair and appropriate for these students? How much do teachers need to know about the cultures of their students—and about their own culture?

Responding to these questions means that we must move beyond the confines of our own, taken for granted ways of doing things, recognise these as culture specific, and expand our understanding of human behaviour to encompass other cultural perspectives and approaches. Chapters 6 and 7 of this book examine some of these issues and propose that, by listening to culture, there are possible directions which can help both teachers and learners.

Peer influence

The peer group may influence emotional or behaviour difficulties in two ways. First, the establishment of positive, reciprocal peer relationships is critical for adaptive social development. Young people who are unable to establish positive peer relationships are at risk, because the peer group is a singularly important positive social dynamic, within which students acquire particular prosocial skills and values. Secondly, the peer group may, by contrast, be able to exert pressure toward negative and maladaptive patterns of behaviour and the acquiring of antisocial values (Kauffman, 1997).

In general, high status or social acceptance is associated with helpfulness, friendliness, and conformity to rules, which in turn leads to prosocial interaction with peers and positive interaction with others. Low status or social rejection is associated with hostility, disruptiveness, and aggression in the peer group (Guevremont & Dumas, 1994; Vercoe, 1998). Low social status among peers is associated with academic failure and a variety of problems in later life, including suicide and delinquency (Langley, Ritchie, & Ritchie, 1996; Sharpe, 1998). Adolescents who are described as chronically delinquent, and have been involved in serious offences such as assault and robbery, present a considerable challenge to school and specialist services personnel. The proliferation of gangs in many communities also poses serious problems for schools, teachers, and members of the community. As natural gathering places for young adolescents, schools may provide both space and opportunity for extortion, drug sales, and other illegal activities associated with gangs. According to Lala (1996) and Mathers (cited in Hardman et al., 1999), young people who lack positive role models, and experience disruptive family structures and economic uncertainty, may seek power, friendship—some form of social acceptance—through gang membership. What defines high status and social acceptance within the gang context is, in the main, contrary to regular and acceptable social norms. However, in many instances gangs are able to provide these young people with some sense of family and personal identity, two core human values which, for many, may not always have been a reality in their lives.

Girish Lala (1996) studied the role of gangs by sharing the experiences of eight former gang members, all of whom were Māori. Seven participants indicated that Māori culture was not important to them or their gangs when they first became members. A significant theme which emerged from Lala's research is summed up by what one gang member, "Joseph", had to say about culture:

> Another part of that new image, which was lost to a lot of members, was their culture, and their identity.... A lot of them don't know who they are; they don't know where they come from; they don't know who their ancestors are; they don't know what canoe they came off and all that stuff. When you don't know that, then really you don't know where you come from to start making progress ... And it was a real shame to the guys. I was one of them. There was part of me that was missing, our culture, and more importantly our mother tongue, Māori. (p. 86)

Māori culture was singled out in Lala's study because of the nature of New Zealand's gangs. From his overview of gang history in New Zealand, he saw that ethnicity has a major impact on the vast majority of gangs in this country.

Before the commencement of his study he thought that it was likely that most participants would identify themselves as Māori. In fact, all the participants did so. Māori culture was a significant factor for many in their pregang lives. However, when they joined gangs, its significance decreased. Once they had left the gangs, for many the significance of culture became important again. There appears to be some congruence in these findings on two counts. First, there is compatibility with the notion that while many Māori are alienated from their Māoritanga, many of their values and spiritual beliefs remain intact (Maniapoto, 1998). On the other hand, previous research carried out on special schools for adolescents with profound behaviour difficulties (Burgess, 1992; Clark, Smith, & Pomare, 1996) showed that, like Joseph in the Lala study, many of the Māori students had failed to achieve a secure identity in their own culture. This failure to achieve a secure identity has negative psychological implications (Erikson, 1968). In the quest for a secure identity, peer influence may come into conflict with other zones of influence, including culture.

Achieving a sense of identity is emphasised because young people tend to behave in ways that are consistent with how they see themselves. Efforts to develop this sense of identity require that students feel accepted by adults such as peers, parents, and teachers. Those who receive constant criticism or rejection tend to see themselves in a negative light, and are apt to be attracted into the company of peers who are experiencing similar identity development crises.

The antidote to negative peer pressure is best summed up by the Māori concept of aroha, meaning love and understanding. Treating young people with respect and establishing a learning environment where individuals know what is expected of them, and where they feel safe, foster aroha. This means having clear rules and expectations and stating these in a consistent manner without intimidating or degrading students. A classroom or school that fosters aroha will enhance goodwill amongst its members; in other words, it helps to build sound peer relations. A lack of aroha has the opposite effect.

Definitions

The need for an acceptable definition of behaviour difficulties is an important prerequisite for accurate identification, appropriate assessment, and programme placement. Varying definitions and ranges of terminology are used in the field of human behaviour; these have emerged from the differing theoretical views appearing in the literature over recent decades. Although arriving at a definition is difficult, establishing one that is suitable for a particular context can be helpful in terms of assessment, programme planning, and placement of students with behaviour difficulties.

The challenges in developing an acceptable definition of behavioural issues have been frequently stated. Kauffman (1997) indicates that the definitional dilemma has been made more difficult by the different conceptual models that have been used in the field (e.g., psychodynamic, biophysical, behavioural, ecological, and sociocultural, as outlined in Chapter 2) and the variety of purposes for definition (e.g., educational, legal, psychological, health related). Although there is no single definition that is acceptable amongst all theorists and practitioners, Bower's (1981) description of severe behaviour disorders has been widely recognised in the field of education:

1. An inability to learn which cannot be explained by intellectual, sensory, or health factors.
2. An inability to build or maintain satisfactory interpersonal relationships with peers and teachers.
3. Inappropriate types of behaviour or feelings under normal conditions.
4. A general pervasive mood of unhappiness or depression.
5. A tendency to develop physical symptoms, pains, or fears associated with personal or school problems. (pp. 115–116)

Bower proposes that an individual is considered to be "behaviourally disordered" if their condition exhibits one or more of these five characteristics over a long period of time and to a marked degree, subsequently affecting educational performance.

Conway (cited in Ashman & Elkins, 2002) puts forward a different but related outline of the defining characteristics of a behaviour disorder, as:

- more than a temporary, unexpected response to stressful events in the environment
- consistently exhibited in two different settings, at least one of which is school related
- persisting despite individualised interventions within the education programme (unless the student's history indicates that such interventions would not be effective). (p. 179)

Although other definitions vary considerably, Hallahan and Kauffman (cited in Fraser, et al., 1995) note that there are some features common to many of them, including:

- behaviour that goes to an extreme; i.e., behaviour that is not just slightly different from that which is perceived as the norm
- a problem that is chronic; one that does not quickly disappear
- behaviour that is unacceptable because of social and cultural expectations.

Such disorders can range from minor to severe, and from transitory to chronic. Andrews and Lupart (1993) consider that teachers should therefore identify behavioural disorders according to their severity, frequency, and chronicity (duration). Moreover, they need to evaluate the behaviour in relation to the developmental level of the student, as well as to social and cultural norms.

So despite the lack of complete consensus about what defines a behaviour disorder, there are certain identifiable features. One reason for it being so difficult to arrive at a reliable definition is that an emotional or behaviour disorder is not something that always exists outside specific social contexts. Instead, emotional or behaviour disorders are labels often assigned according to rules chosen by certain authority figures (Peterson & Ishii-Jordan, 1994). Typically, it is behaviour that is perceived to threaten the stability, security, or values of a particular society (Moynihan, cited in Kauffman, 1997).

As problematic as establishing a definition may be, it remains too important to leave to chance. The definition which is accepted is important in terms of how the problem is conceptualised, and this helps when considering appropriate intervention strategies. Definitions communicate conceptual frameworks that have direct implications for practitioners: medical definitions imply the need for medical assessment and interventions; educational definitions imply the need for educational assessments and interventions; and so on (Kauffman, 1997).

A continuum of behaviour difficulties

From an ecological perspective, a behaviour difficulty is generally described as a situation of conflict between the student and the environment, in ways which deviate significantly from age-appropriate expectations. This situation interferes with the learning of the student, and with the learning of others. A number of studies (Conway, 1998; Porter, 1996; Wheldall & Merrett, 1989) have qualitatively described these behaviours along a continuum from mild to severe. These studies lend support to the way Charles (1999) categorises different types of such misbehaviour, along with their severity and level of prevalence:

> Teachers concur with five broad *types of misbehaviour*. In descending order of seriousness, as judged by social scientists, they are as follows:

1. Aggression: physical and verbal attacks on the teacher or other students.
2. Immorality: acts such as cheating, lying, and stealing.
3. Defiance of authority: refusal, sometimes hostile, to do as the teacher requests.
4. Class disruptions: talking loudly, calling out, walking about the room, clowning, tossing objects.
5. Goofing off: fooling around, out of seat, not doing assigned tasks, dawdling, daydreaming. (p. 2)

According to Charles (1999), there is general concurrence amongst researchers and teachers that the most dreaded behaviours that teachers face in schools are aggression, immorality, and defiance. But he also points out that teachers seldom encounter these types of behaviours. It is the less serious behaviours, such as goofing off and inattention, that are far more prevalent. These apparently innocuous, repetitive behaviours not only stress teachers to the point where their responses may often be counterproductive, but they are also the behaviours that waste instructional time, and therefore interfere with learning.

That said, the notion that teachers seldom have to deal with the more serious behaviours is now being challenged. In New Zealand, according to Liberty, Clark, and Solomon (2000) there is an estimated incidence of severe problems in 3 percent of children, and moderate problems in 4–6 percent of children. They contend that this would be approximately 34,000 primary school children. According to Moore, Anderson, and Sharma (2006), internationally, schools are reported to be resorting increasingly to suspension and expulsion, as a way of dealing with the growing issue of severe misbehaviour. Meyer and Evans (2006) suggest that it can be argued that the presence of such challenging behaviours is a growing problem internationally, and refer to an escalating number of media reports and television programmes that present case studies of children with severe behaviour problems.

Despite the difficulty of achieving a general consensus about what constitutes a behaviour disorder, it is possible to identify a number of clusters of behaviours, each of which has recognisable features. These clusters can be represented in a behaviour continuum (see Table 3.1). The location of the student on the behaviour continuum has a significant bearing on who introduces the intervention strategy, and what form the strategy is likely to take. "Although universal school-wide support efforts are sufficient for most students, some children need more specialized and intensive supports" (Sugai, 2003, p. 530).

Table 3.1 The behaviour continuum

1 Mild/Moderate	2 Severe	3 Serious
Displays adjustment difficulty and often fails to respond to usual range of management strategies. Talks out of turn and hinders other students.	Is judged by more than one authoritative adult to be severely excessive, deficient or inappropriate within given social situations.	Interferes seriously with either the student's or other people's wellbeing, learning and teaching, and continues at an unacceptable level, subsequent to intervention which has been implemented accurately and with integrity. Defiant, violent, uncouth.

Adapted from Conway, cited in Ashman and Elkins (1998).

Level 1 behaviours are those that interfere with the orderly environment of the classroom. Responses to these more commonly occurring behaviours are usually implemented by the teacher and/or RTLB. They should be developmentally appropriate, instructive, and positive.

Level 2 behaviours are those that interfere with the orderly environment of the school, and are potentially dangerous to the wellbeing of the student and staff. The teacher, senior staff member(s), school counsellor, and GSE worker are likely to be involved in implementing responses to these behaviours. Notification of parents will often be necessary.

Level 3 behaviours are considered the most serious violations, and represent a direct threat to the orderly operation of the classroom or school. More specialised personnel from GSE and/or another community agency group are likely to be involved in implementing responses to these behaviours. It may be necessary to exclude the student for a period of time that is commensurate with the seriousness of the behaviour.

Summary

This chapter addresses four influential environments (family, school, culture, and peers), discusses the problematic nature of definition, and introduces the types of behaviour that regularly occur in classrooms and schools. The reason for presenting these sets of factors is twofold. One is to present a case that is persuasive enough to convince teachers that some knowledge of the origins and interpretations of behaviour difficulties is extremely useful in guiding the management of the behaviour(s). The other is so that teachers have a clearer idea that the influencing environments, the definition of behaviour difficulties, and the types of behaviour difficulties are a spiralling clutch of interrelated concepts (Goodlad, 1997). It does not seem possible to look at each in isolation.

This chapter provides an outline of each of the interrelated concepts and the clear message to all professionals in the field is that it is not unwise to look at the broad picture before attending to the detail. From the respective environments of family, school, culture, and peers, important links may be made to the onset of behaviour difficulties, and their potential to intensify or diminish. It must also be noted that the definition of these behaviour difficulties is a matter complicated by differences in the conceptual models (such as those outlined in Chapter 2), the transience of the behaviour difficulties, and the effects of labelling of many of these students. While no definition has met with universal acceptance, the most common one used in educational contexts is that proposed by Bower (1981). The markers of this definition are characteristics pertaining to the following:
- school learning problems
- unsatisfactory interpersonal relationships
- inappropriate behaviour and feelings
- pervasive unhappiness or depression
- physical symptoms or fears associated with school or personal problems.

Five broad types of behaviour are introduced in this chapter: aggression, immorality, defiance, disruption, and goofing. These behaviours are illustrated, in terms of their prevalence and severity across a continuum.

Students who present with challenging behaviours often experience difficulties in relating effectively to peers, teachers, and parents. They also have difficulty responding to academic and social tasks, the core areas of their education. It is important therefore, that educators have a sound understanding of the various influences that explain and help us to understand the sources of the problems, the types of behaviours that exist, and why definitions of behaviour difficulties are necessary.

PART

TWO

TRAVERSING THE BEHAVIOUR CONTINUUM

Strategies for responding to varying levels of behaviour difficulties

4 **Landmark developments in classroom management:** strategies for responding to mild to moderate behaviour difficulties

5 **Students on track at Railway School:** strategies for dealing with severe behaviour difficulties

CHAPTER 4

Landmark developments in classroom management:
strategies for responding to mild to moderate behaviour difficulties

Introduction

Although the word *discipline* is in constant use in the teaching profession, it is not always the preferred term. For some years, *classroom management* has been seen as less offensive, and thus more in vogue. According to Lefrancois (1988), part of the reason for this lies in current philosophical movements in education:

> To the extent that discipline has been equated with yesterday's teacher, and to the extent that the activities most often associated with disciplinary measures are interpreted as being incompatible with the more permissive, more humanistic, and more child-centered beliefs of the present age, it has seemed more appropriate to exhort teachers to 'manage' their classrooms rather than to 'discipline' them. (p. 288)

Discipline is both a noun and a verb. As a noun, discipline can be understood to mean orderliness; as a verb, it can be understood to mean to put to right. If these interpretations are considered to be fair, then one should feel at ease using either term to describe a particular context, and to illuminate a variety of methods that might be employed to maintain a classroom climate conducive to learning and to the appropriate social development of children and young people. Discipline thus encompasses procedural strategies, instructional strategies, incentives and disincentives, reinforcers, and other facets of teacher–learner interaction.

Lefrancois (1988) notes that while the terms discipline and classroom management are often matched, there is nevertheless an important difference between the two. Stated succinctly, classroom management refers to the arrangement of the classroom activities in order to facilitate learning and teaching. Discipline refers to the ways in which teachers respond to and manage student behaviours that disrupt (or threaten to disrupt) classroom activities. Thus, management and disciplinary functions may occur simultaneously, or in close sequence, in relation to a particular action or event in the classroom. Both discipline and classroom management are integral to the ongoing process of teaching and learning.

This chapter considers several classroom management and disciplinary strategies that have emerged from early scholarship, and argues that these strategies continue to be a vehicle for establishing a positive classroom climate where students feel valued and motivated. It also argues that fundamental to student motivation is effective communication, based on positive and reciprocal teacher and student relationships. Positive relationships are in turn integral to effective classroom management, because the particular strategies a teacher employs are more likely to be successful in a climate of mutual respect.

The dual role of the classroom teacher

Beveridge (1995) insists that the extent to which teachers demonstrate genuine interest in young people as individuals, as well as care and concern for the class as a whole, is reflected in their planning, organisation, and management of learning experiences. This calls on teachers to have a dual role in the classroom, referred to by Doyle (1986) as an instructional function and a managerial function. Briefly, the instructional function helps the teacher to cover the prescribed curriculum, to ensure mastery of content, and to promote favourable attitudes to the subject in particular and the curriculum in general. The managerial function requires that the teacher promotes order through social constructs, procedures, rules, and by responding effectively to behaviour issues when they arise. Smith and Laslett (1993) have also written about management rather than control of a classroom. They refer to management as skilled organisation and lesson presentation that actively engages students in learning. These rules are listed here in a very abbreviated format, and with a slight modification to phraseology and the original order:

- Get them in: greeting, seating, starting. Simply by being there to receive students is a sign of the teacher's authority and sense of purpose. Age of the students and the nature of the activity will determine the room plan, but student placement and control of movement are determined by the teacher. Starting promptly and decisively sets the scene and establishes a positive tone before moving on to the main content of the lesson.
- Get on with it: content, manner. Difficulties in learning and consequent difficulties with behaviour often happen because the content of a lesson is not matched to the ability of those to whom it is delivered. Therefore, finding out what students already know and planning small steps toward respective goals are useful strategies. The lesson should maintain momentum and have variety in terms of pace and pitch. Teacher manner is related to the concept of "withitness" (Kounin, 1977) wherein a smooth flow is maintained and disciplinary disruptions are avoided.
- Get on with them: who's who, what's going on—knowing each child as an individual and reading the mood of the class as a whole. Knowing students' names and getting the right pronunciation are testimony to personalised learning that adds to the teacher's mana. Scan the room and "work the crowd"—two simple but powerful strategies to help the teacher know what's going on and be more responsive to the prevailing mood of the group.
- Move them on: closing, dismissing, and transitioning. Though most disciplinary problems arise from a poor start to a lesson, the next most vulnerable time providing opportunities for behaviour difficulties is at the end of a teaching session. A good lesson could be ruined if allowed to dissolve into a noisy, topsy-turvy finale. Orderly procedures for concluding should include signalling that there are so many minutes to go. The teacher should identify some revision points, make some reiteration of key concepts, and offer some reaffirmation for less competent students so that the possibility for pleasure and enjoyment will not be extinguished.

Arthur, Gordon, and Butterfield (2003) reason that while the learning process is highly individual and personal for students, the way in which the teacher manages the learning environment is critical in terms of the quality of learning that takes place, as well as the attitudes that students develop in relation to themselves as learners and to their teachers as teachers. The learning environment is made up of the three interwoven systems of classroom, school, and community (Senge et al., 2000). The classroom is the core of these; it is a space populated by one adult (except for team teaching) and by many students, with a host of different activities occurring at the same time. In a sense, it is multidimensional. For the teacher, there is often little time for reflection, and thinking on your feet is a regular occurrence.

The classroom is an unpredictable place, where a combination of human mannerisms, interactions, and natural elements can determine the mood within its walls. All the while, the actions of individual students and teachers are on show. This type of "publicness" has significant implications for behaviour; both appropriate and inappropriate behaviours can become contagious. The classroom is also a place where each member brings with them part of their previous histories and experiences (Doyle, 1986).

Teachers therefore have to call on a range of particular qualities, including attitudes, skills, knowledge, and experience. According to Jensen (1995), a further quality, acumen, describes the high professional standards that good teachers set for themselves. This includes: learning about the various cultures represented in the classroom; discovering what has been done by other teachers in the past; looking through school archives; and asking colleagues and community members about the local traditions, rituals, and legends. Developing this acumen is in line with Blumberg's (1989) notion of developing a nose for things—having a sense of process.

Why straightforward interventions matter

Developing a nose for things and having a sense of process is not a guarantee that disruptive behaviours will not occur in the classroom, or will be able to be significantly alleviated if they do occur. Indeed, there are such things as enemies of quality instructional time. In a classic study, Wheldall and Merrett (1989) reported on the types of behaviour difficulties experienced in schools in the West Midlands in the United Kingdom (UK). These researchers were keen to identify the types of behaviours that teachers found most troublesome. They questioned 198 primary teachers and received replies from 32 schools. There was a remarkable consensus among the respondents that "talking out of turn" and "hindering other children" (affectionately referred to as TOOT and HOC) were the most troublesome and the most frequent behaviours in classrooms—the chief enemies to quality instructional time.

Teachers in the study reported that when teachers' attention was directed towards children described as particularly troublesome, they identified a range of behaviours, such as disobedience, idleness, and physical aggression. One of the most significant aspects of this study was that more than half the teachers responded that they spent more time than they ought to do on the issue of order and control, and that this amounted to immense time wasting. Wheldall and Merrett arrived at a compelling conclusion: straightforward interventions by teachers can bring about dramatic results in terms of improved classroom atmosphere and the quantity and quality of work produced. Successfully implemented, such interventions also yield a more satisfying and rewarding classroom experience for both teachers and students.

Landmark studies

It has been close to fifty years since educators began actively searching for ways to promote acceptable student behaviour by employing means other than intimidation and punishment. In the last thirty years, discipline has risen to the top of the list of teacher concerns. Some of the pioneers in this field included Fritz Redl and William Wattenberg, whose focus was on group behaviour and exploring how individual behaviour within groups could be more easily understood and managed. B. F. Skinner followed in the 1960s employing, primarily, the shaping of desired student behaviour through the principles of reinforcement (Charles, 1999).

Many notable research studies and publications followed, including Jacob Kounin's landmark studies on behaviour management through lesson control, and Fredric Jones's *Positive Classroom Discipline* (1987), which has been in use since 1979, and continues to attract a large following. Table 4.1 lists some of the contributors to the field, along with the fundamental propositions that underpin their respective works. The most thorough analyses of many of these landmark studies is provided by C. M. Charles in *Building Classroom Discipline* (1999), now into its seventh edition.

A contribution from Jacob Kounin

Jacob Kounin's work is cited in most writings about classroom management, and his ideas have been included in many of the application models and in many locations (Charles, 2002). The scholarship carried out by Kounin in the 1970s is considered a landmark study of classroom management. This study involved videotaping hundreds of classrooms which varied in the extent of control that the teacher had established. Kounin examined these recordings, expecting to find differences in the way these teachers dealt with discipline

Table 4.1 Landmark developments in classroom management

Contributors	Fundamental propositions about discipline
Fritz Redl and William Wattenburg	Understanding *group dynamics* is critical. Group expectations strongly influence behaviour, and vice versa. Recognition of causes precedes effective intervention.
Jacob Kounin	Champions the notion of *withitness*—knowing what is going on at all times. Key aspects include teacher organisation, lesson presentation, classroom arrangement, and smooth transitions.
Haim Ginott	Promotion of self-discipline in small steps, over time, based on the power of *congruent communication*, is fundamental to this approach.
B.F. Skinner	The principles of *applied behaviour analysis* have their origins here. Skinnerians advocate for the gradual *Shaping* of acceptable behaviour through reinforcement, with emphasis on successive approximations.
Lee and Marlene Canter	*Assertive discipline*, an applied approach wherein teachers have a right to teach without disruption, and students have a right to a safe, calm, and supportive environment.
Fredric Jones	The introduction of positive classroom discipline that espouses *effective body language* and adroit incentive systems, is central to this approach.
William Glasser	*Quality education* in the curriculum, teaching and learning is the focus of this "lead" rather than "boss" approach for meeting students' basic needs in a noncoercive way.
Herbert Grossman	The ideas are premised on empowering teachers to select techniques that suit their own personalities, philosophies, and values, while *accommodating diverse backgrounds*.
Janice Wearmouth, Ted Glynn, and Mere Berryman	*Belonging* is the underpinning focus. With appropriate support, students can adapt and respond positively within a learning environment where they are valued, respected, and feel that they belong.

problems. He was surprised to find very few differences. Whether they had sound or inadequate control strategies, teachers reacted to disruptions in much the same way.

This prompted Kounin to re-examine the videos and to look more analytically at the particular teaching methods and classroom organisational strategies. What he discovered was to become the central discourse of his work. He found that the methods used by those teachers who displayed sound control increased the amount of on-task behaviour in students. Because students were more productively engaged, fewer disruptions occurred.

In order to implement sound classroom management, lessons and activities need to be well prepared, soundly organised, and presented in a way that is cognitively relevant and motivating. Arthur et al. (2003) and Charles (1999, 2002) noted that Kounin's principles of effective teaching included several key components. Teachers who had sound control:

- displayed "withitness" by regularly scanning the class for disruptions, and planning for variation in activities
- were able to "overlap", meaning that they were capable of attending to several things at once
- maintained momentum, so that they started a lesson with dispatch, maintaining the momentum, bringing it to a satisfactory close, and making the smooth transition from one activity to the next; maintaining smoothness or involvement in this way enhanced steady progression without abruptness or disturbing incidents
- had systems for gaining attention, also known as "group alerting"
- employed "the ripple effect": as a consequence of reprimanding one student, others also changed their behaviour.

By using the ideas and methods inherent in Kounin's discipline model, teachers are able to be better positioned to keep their students on task and focused. His model, like others in the field, proposes that challenging behaviours are reduced by engaging students and offering a variety of activities, thereby making learning more meaningful and interesting.

Kounin's model offers suggestions for preventing mild to moderate challenging behaviours occurring in the classroom, but not necessarily for providing strategies to deal with serious problems when they arise (Morris, 1996). However, in the final analysis, Kounin's contribution to the literature on school discipline and classroom management warrants serious attention. When these strategies are appropriately implemented, they are economical, efficient, and effective.

A contribution from Fredric Jones

Fredric Jones (1987), the developer of *Positive Classroom Discipline*, was the first to devote attention to the role of nonverbal communication in promoting classroom discipline. According to Charles (2002), Jones worked for many years to develop training procedures for improving teacher effectiveness in motivating, managing, and instructing students. Since the early 1970s, Jones and his colleagues, from Santa Cruz in California, have spent thousands of hours observing and recording data in hundreds of elementary and secondary classrooms. Jones's work has been influenced by classroom management methods employed by highly successful teachers, especially those methods associated with keeping students on task, providing individual help when needed, and dealing with misbehaviour.

As in Wheldall and Merrett's (1989) UK study, Jones found that massive time-wasting was due to student behaviours such as talking out of turn, goofing off, and moving around the room without permission. However, he found very little defiance—the behaviour that teachers dread. Therefore it seemed logical to address the common behaviours that often leave teachers feeling frustrated and defeated. Jones emphasises that the most successful way to manage unacceptable behaviour is to prevent it from happening in the first place. The best mode of prevention, he proposes, is to provide a cluster of skills designed around a classroom structure. This set of skills pays specific attention to room arrangement, class rules, class chores, and routines for beginning class. It includes:

- Room arrangement: minimise the physical distance, so that the teacher can "work the crowd".
- Classroom rules: a few general rules to define the broad guidelines, and some specific rules describing routines and how to do them: teach these early in the year and rehearse them.
- Classroom chores: these give students a sense of ownership and responsibility.
- Opening routines: keep notices to a minimum and "get on with it".

(Jones, cited in Charles, 1999, p. 109)

Jones then proposes a second cluster of skills which have the capacity to define boundaries through body language. These include:

- Remain calm: when attending to a behaviour matter, maintain self-control. A calm teacher conveys strength and rationality.
- Eye contact: teachers need to practise this skill to get it right. Scan the room to get a feel for the classroom landscape. Engage the eyes of an individual student when necessary. The direct (brief) look by the teacher tells the students that their behaviour, both good and bad, is being noted. Cultural sensitivity must be considered.

- Proximity control: move closer to where the unacceptable behaviour is occurring, make brief eye contact, and say nothing. In almost all instances, the student will immediately revert to behaviour that is appropriate.
- Body carriage: this is an effective way of communicating the teacher's confidence and authority—or their lack. Effective teachers, whatever their mood, tend to hold themselves straight and move with composure.
- Facial expression: this strategy sends the message to the students about their teacher's enthusiasm, seriousness, enjoyment—and so encourages appropriate behaviour. An unpleasant facial expression achieves the opposite effect. (Jones, cited in Charles, 1999, pp. 110–111)

By using ideas and methods inherent in the Jones discipline model, teachers should be better positioned to maximise instructional time in the classroom. This approach also suggests that teachers combine body language with an incentive system to control behaviour problems.

According to Morris (1996), there are advantages and disadvantages to the Jones approach to discipline:

> The Jones model appears advantageous because it specifies a set of steps or activities to follow when dealing with discipline problems. This can be very helpful to teachers because it provides structure for their activities. Also, this model encourages teachers, administrators, and parents to work together to combat discipline problems.
>
> A major disadvantage of the Jones model is that student independence is not encouraged. For example, Jones emphasizes the importance of creating seating charts in which the student does not have the option of choosing a seat. Furthermore, the suggested use of body language may embarrass teachers and make students uncomfortable if taken to extremes. (p. 11)

Communication is a complex, two-way process that involves a diverse array of interplay and execution. Jones explains the process with clarity, and gives meaning to particular concepts in a way that provides inspiration for teachers to both adopt and adapt the strategies. Once mastered, these strategies have the potential to make the teacher a consummate and artful practitioner.

Preventing mild to moderate behaviour difficulties: discipline as a noun

We have seen that there are a number of basic approaches that teachers can use in the classroom to reduce the incidence of mild to moderate behaviour difficulties. Teachers who establish sound classroom routines and have clear expectations of their students are minimising opportunities for potential problems to occur. They are therefore actively engaged in reducing potential stress. These precursory steps, also known as antecedents, are simple but powerful strategies.

A second approach teachers can take is a problem-solving one. This approach is intended to increase the students' abilities to deal more effectively with problem situations. For example, a teacher who holds classroom meetings to facilitate students solving their own problems promotes their ability and competence to deal with similar problems in the future.

Intervening early in order to prevent behaviour difficulties requires focusing on the antecedents of behaviour. Students who are vulnerable to behaviour difficulties have weaker coping skills in dealing with some of the intricacies of classroom activities and expectations. There are a number of conditions and situations that represent the most significant risks for students, in terms of increasing the chances of difficult behaviour occurring. These include unstructured activities, delays and interruptions in routines and activities, academic tasks that are boring or demotivating, and so forth.

The teacher who structures his or her classroom and instructional environment to avoid or reduce these hazards will have taken an important stride towards preventing an increase in behaviour difficulties. These teachers are the good planners, good organisers, and effective communicators. They deal with discipline as a noun; they manage the classroom well to facilitate learning and teaching.

Responding to mild to moderate behaviour difficulties: discipline as a verb

As Bill Rogers (1997) asserts, there are no guarantees in behaviour management. There will be times when a form of discipline is required. This requires teachers to deal with discipline as a verb. This form of discipline involves putting matters to right by responding to behaviours that disrupt classroom activities. Selected examples of how to respond to tricky situations follow.

At this juncture in this chapter, a range of scenarios and practical intervention strategies will be outlined and explained. The justification for this diversion in the tone and style of the writing is that teachers are enthusiastic to be introduced to intervention techniques that work—they prefer explanations that are punchy and lucid. According to Lewis (1997) teachers seem to be interested in the assertive techniques of Canter and Canter (1992), the behaviour recovery approaches advocated by Bill Rogers (1990) and David Wright (1998), and in the ideas that emerge from the work of William Glasser (1992), Maurice Balson (1992), and others. The work of these writers is hereby acknowledged. Macfarlane (1997, 2002, 2003, 2004) and Bateman (2003, 2007) now offer examples that draw from their own teaching experiences and research activities, and that simultaneously encapsulate many of the notions espoused by the Canters and other noted contributors in the field.

Talking during quiet work time

When students begin to talk in low voices during silent work time, remind them that this is a quiet activity and talking may prevent others from concentrating on their work:

> Teacher: This is a quiet activity time, so there will be no talking. Raise your hand if you wish to talk to me, thank you.

Do not make confrontational statements such as "Stop talking!" Resist the temptation to ask the question, "What are you talking about?" This will effectively give students permission to talk further, and enable them to defend their position by responding that they were talking about an aspect of their work.

This example reiterates the significance of taking preventive measures. The most successful strategy is to minimise opportunities in the first place. One strategy is to establish a whole-class "noise level register" at the beginning of the year. Discuss why some activities require silence (a level "zero" setting), why others are suited to quiet talking/low voices (a level 1 setting), and why normal talking voices (a level 2 setting) are suitable for the remainder. At the beginning of each activity, write the setting you require in the noise level register space on the whiteboard, and reiterate the expectation verbally. Reinforce adherence to the setting in a quiet voice as you move around the room. It is also important to not set a level zero setting for an unreasonably extended period of time. Therefore be observant of restlessness; when this begins, raise the level to a 1 or 2 and have some focused interactive discussion, relevant to the activity, for a period of time.

Class unrest at the start of the period: entering the class

From time to time students may feel that it is acceptable to enter a room, or begin an activity, with a lot of unnecessary noise and bravado. This behaviour must be addressed in very short order so that expectations are clearly reiterated and maintained. Failure to do so could well lead to unacceptable habits being established. Be immediate, be assertive, be succinct:

Teacher: Listen up. That is not the way we conduct ourselves in this class. The right way, as you know, is to enter quietly, sit down, and prepare to start.

The tone of the teacher's voice will denote a sense of assertiveness, and the restating of expectations clearly reminds students that compliance is required. This type of behaviour does not call for a severe reprimand. Reprimands should be used sparingly, specifically, and privately.

If the noise persists, however, and the students appear unsettled, direct the class outside to line up in an orderly way. A statement such as "OK, let's try that again shall we—everyone line up quietly outside the door—thank you" will indicate that compliance is required, and reaffirm expectations. Go out with them and explain how you expect them to behave. Articulate three behaviours that you will be observing, and that you expect a 100 percent result: "Walk in calmly, sit down, and wait quietly—thank you." Avoid threats such as whole-class detentions or lunchtime practices of the expected behaviour. Instead, get them back in the room and seated, remind them about the rule, and discuss the standard with them. Be brief and definitive, and then move on.

Class unrest at the beginning of an activity: getting started

Sometimes students will be unsettled at the beginning of an activity, and this will make the process of starting a lesson very difficult. Transition from one activity or lesson to another is an example of when this may happen. Preparing students in advance about when an activity will end—and how—is essential; however, there may still be times when unrest may appear, despite your best efforts. One strategy that is fun to use, and excellent for redirecting potential escalation of unrest, is a sudden and snappy game. This needs to be introduced and used previously when the class is settled, so that they perceive it as a positive teacher interaction, and will also know what they need to do upon hearing a particular prompt. Possible teacher prompts include:
- teacher claps a pattern loudly, and the students echo it
- teacher sings a tune and the students echo it
- teacher sings part of a funny ditty and the students finish it
- teacher whistles a tune and the students sing it back using the words
- teacher hums a tune and the students sing it back using the words.

This strategy effectively distracts students from escalating unrest. Once their collective attention and focus is regained, a quiet voice can be used to set a quiet and calm tone.

Not having the right items

Despite the best of intentions, students may sometimes forget or ignore instructions to bring materials or completed work to class. The responsibility of completing homework, packing the right PE gear, bringing money for a school trip, etc., does not rest with the student alone, but often with parents and caregivers. When students forget something that they have been asked to bring to school, a contingency plan is required so that they do not miss out on what was planned for them.

Preventive measures include sending a letter home to parents/caregivers in advance. Timing is important: they may forget if the letter is sent too early, or not have sufficient time to prepare if it is sent too late. Have students make a note of any requirements, as the act of writing them down may well help commit them to memory. A home–school contact book is a useful resource. Have spaces in the notebook for parents to sign, comment, or both. Clearly, pre-empting issues is the most effective way of solving them. Get in early. Reinforce appropriate behaviours; do not emphasise inappropriate behaviours. Have some spare sets of materials and resources ready just in case.

However, when students continually forget to bring the right materials for class activities, further demands are placed on the teacher, therefore responding and managing these situations is critical. During teaching time is not the best context for sorting out these problems, so communication with parents/caregivers may be necessary to determine the reasons. If it is clear that family resources are being stretched beyond capacity, or are indeed unable to cater for the materials that are required at school, then respectful management needs to include upholding the esteem and status of the student in front of his or her peers. Once again, a ready supply of materials and resources is essential, and supplying these to the student needs to be done quietly and without fuss. Occasionally it may even be necessary to be somewhat mischievous. For example:

> Teacher: These (articles of clothing) were dropped off from home for you earlier, possibly from home, Michael.
> (In fact they were supplied from another source.)

This strategy may be used to protect the student and his/her family from derision. Speak privately with the student about this later so that they are aware of what has happened and why.

Low-level swearing

Students will swear at various times. It is important to determine the reason, and the target. For example, a student drops a drink bottle and exclaims, "This p----- me right off!" This is clearly expressing a level of frustration; it is not directed at anyone in particular and is therefore unlikely to require a heavy-handed response. The best strategy is to tactically ignore it. Depending on how widely it has been heard and how much it intrigues or unsettles the rest of the class, however, a low-level response may be necessary. Stopping and looking in the direction of the student may be enough. Stopping, looking, and adding a focused "ahem" in the direction of the students may also be all that is required. Similarly, use a statement such as: "I hope I did not hear any swearing just now—I'm sure I didn't." Later, you could mention to the student in private that while dropping the bottle was indeed annoying (empathise initially), inappropriate language is not an option at school. To make an issue of this behaviour publicly would merely draw attention to something that does not require further reinforcement. It would also disrupt the teaching or the activity if it happened during class time.

Choosing not to engage in class work or activities

Students choosing not to engage is something that irritates teachers, because it presents as passive resistance (a form of defiance) that might expose a vulnerability in the teacher. This form of behaviour, if not handled properly, has the potential to escalate into behaviours that are far more severe, seriously disrupting other students—possibly the classroom as a whole. In addition, it may do lasting damage to the student–teacher relationship, as well as to the student's own educational success.

There are three main types of nonengagement: defiance, avoidance, and anxiety. It is important to be sure which type it is when implementing a strategy. Strategies for responding to all three types are relatively similar, and involve progressing through a set of three steps. Steps one and three are the same across all types of nonengagement; however, step two is quite specific to each type. Table 4.2 below gives an overview of the three types of nonengagement, as well as a brief outline of the steps that need to be followed by the teacher. A brief example for each type of nonengagement follows.

Table 4.2 Strategies for responding to student nonengagement

	Defiance Not responding to simple requirements	**Avoidance** Choosing to opt out, for no apparent reason	**Anxiety** Emotional or social influences driving non-engagement
Step one	← **Strategy**: planned ignoring of student **Focus**: whole class: praise, incentive →		
Step two	**Strategy**: Implication that compliance is already happening Reinforce accordingly Encourage them to "continue" Reiterate incentive Leave student to start **Focus**: proximity One-to-one Indirect	**Strategy**: Implication that compliance will eventuate Encourage, motivate Provide direct help and assistance Help student to get started Define individual work requirement Provide ongoing, timely assistance **Focus**: proximity One-to-one Direct	**Strategy**: Implication that compliance will eventuate Encourage, affirm, express warmth Help student to get started Provide "special" help and assistance Outline work requirement Leave student to work **Focus**: proximity One-to-one Direct
Step three	← **Strategy**: choices provided; consequences outlined **Focus**: one-to-one: direct →		

Defiance

Nonengagement defiance irritates teachers a great deal. It directly challenges teachers by conveying the message: "I can do what I want—you can take it or leave it!" The secret is to remain calm, and to ignore it in the first instance.

Step one: Use encouraging and affirmative comments to reinforce and clarify your expectations of all the students, and the tasks that are required of them:

> Teacher: *(Is aware that a student is sitting there with his or her arms crossed, or muttering that they are not going to do the work.)*
> Well done class! I like the way you all are getting into this work! Remember, this has to be completed by 11 o'clock and it looks like that won't be a problem! We might get a game in this afternoon if this effort is maintained. If anyone needs help, raise your hand.

Continue to ignore the behaviour, as the nonengaged student is highly likely to begin the task at that point. If not, move on to the next step:

Step two: Use proximity (plus a quiet and calm voice), imply that the student has made a start (perhaps by way of thinking), and offer a favourable comment accordingly:

> Teacher: You're still thinking, right? Good one! I'll be back in a minute or two and see how you are going. Carry on. Looking forward to the game later!

Allow one or two minutes before returning to the scene: usually step two will prompt the student to engage. If it does not have the desired effect, it is important to implement the next step:

Step three: Remain calm and unemotional; clearly articulate what it is that the student is expected to do. Be unobtrusive so as to not draw attention to the situation. Offer a choice, mention a possible consequence, and leave the scene:

> Teacher: You won't meet the 11 o'clock deadline if you keep doing all of this thinking for too much longer! Better that you get started now. If you need help, I'm here.
>
> Remember the deadline ... or the work will need to be finished this afternoon while the class goes out for that game I mentioned. I think Mrs Thorpe in Room 12 won't mind you using her room. Come on now—we need you to do one of those big hits again!

This statement gives the student the choice between (a) completing a task during class time with the opportunity of participating in a game, or (b) having to complete a set task outside of class time, but missing out on a game. More often than not, students will favour the former option. This means that disruption and/or confrontation is avoided, and the responsibility for managing their behaviour is handed back to the student. Obviously the consequence would need to be carried out if the resistance continued.

Avoidance

Task avoidance can manifest for several reasons. It may be that a student does not understand what is required of them, they may not be able to do what is required of them, or they might not like or be interested in what is required of them. As mentioned under defiance, **step one** needs to be implemented at the outset. But if this does not work, the response at **step two** needs to be tailored in response to avoidance. This could be as follows:

Step two:

> Teacher: So you are still thinking—that's fine! Where is your book? Right, let me see what you might do … you put the date on there (*wait there*)—good—now let's talk about what you've been thinking about. What was a major cause of the disaster on the Titanic? Give me a brief explanation. If you had been there, what would you have …

The secret here is to help, to encourage, and to build on their ideas, by using questions and positive comments. It may also be necessary to write down their ideas, to talk them through, and then ask that they write their ideas (as transcribed by you, the teacher) into their book. It may also be appropriate to let them know that you will be back in a few minutes to carry on with the work once they have finished that part. **Step three** may or may not need to be introduced, depending on their compliance levels.

Emotional or social nonengagement

Nonengagement that stems from emotional or social factors needs to be handled sensitively. What happens to a student outside the classroom is often reflected in how they respond within it. Placing extra pressure on, or confronting, a student who is attempting to deal with some kind of strongly negative emotion or with trauma, abuse, neglect, intimidation, or bullying is not going to benefit anyone. Indeed, it may merely serve to further damage their self-esteem and self-efficacy. Care and sensitivity, therefore, are essential. Once again, **step one** needs to be used at the outset. The student may actually decide to start work at that point, but if this does not happen, then **step two** needs to be modified. The teacher needs to gauge and determine what is reasonable and fair to require of the student, given their emotional state. Note the use of the pronoun "we" in the following example:

> Teacher: I see that you're still thinking, that's great! Let's talk about what might be a good idea … what we might do. I'm really interested in your ideas! Let's try this, you talk and I write. We'll make this into a choice piece of work. Don't let anyone else in on this yet. We'll surprise them!

The intention of responding in this way is to provide the student with a sense of agency; to encourage them, to let them know that you are keen to listen, and to show that you value them; their contributions and ideas. It is essential that the teacher further avoids adding to the anxiety or possible trauma that the student may be experiencing. Being realistic about what it is that you expect from them in terms of output, given their perceived emotional state, is imperative. It may also be necessary to follow up further as to the cause(s) of their emotional and/or social plight.

Low-level verbal put-downs

Put-downs need to be handled expeditiously and appropriately by teachers. It is imperative that teachers neither collude with this form of bullying, nor model it in their own behaviours and interactions. Promoting a culture of care, tolerance, inclusion, and respect within classrooms will indicate to students what teacher expectations might be, in terms of both verbal and nonverbal communications and interactions.

Low-level verbal put-downs are sometimes dismissed by teachers as normal student banter, and this may be so in some instances. However, sometimes what might appear to be innocent chatter may actually be more subtle or insidious. Therefore, paying close attention to the sorts of verbal (and nonverbal) interactions that are regularly occurring between and amongst students needs to be a part of a class-wide assessment and management process.

For example, a group of students is sitting together. The teacher overhears Student A joking to the other students about Student B's shoes as he walks past:

Student A: Hey Jace; where'd you get your budget shoes from, man! The Warehouse? Ha ha… (*Student A laughs—as do the other students.*)

Student B: Yeah! (*Student B laughs briefly, but uncomfortably.*)

It sounds light-hearted, and no-one gets visibly agitated, or appears to be upset; but the astute teacher becomes aware by the look on Student B's face that it is not something that he feels totally comfortable with. This situation needs to be handled swiftly and carefully; the response needs to clearly indicate that comments such as these are not at all appropriate, nor are they to be encouraged. By ignoring such comments, the teacher may indirectly indicate that it is actually normal and proper to speak like that to other people, thereby colluding with the inappropriate comments. The response, however, needs to be delivered in a light-hearted and semibemused manner, and to lead quickly toward a totally different matter. Notice that the teacher does not even need to single out or refer to either Student A or Student B:

Teacher: (*In a fun tone—light-heartedly*) Whoa! So what's wrong with the Warehouse then!! That's my favourite shop—all the trendy people shop there eh! Love the shoes! (*changing the subject*) Hey, are you guys going to be at practice tomorrow? By the way, it's 3.30, not 4.30 …

It is important that the teacher does not respond in an over-the-top or confrontational way to Student A, for two reasons. First, this type of "buy in" reaction is unnecessary. Secondly, it would actually model the inappropriate behaviour which the teacher is concerned about. Such a response is also likely to damage the relationship that the teacher has built up with Student A. Another outcome that is very often overlooked is that by admonishing Student A so publicly, the teacher may actually be alienating Student B from his peers. Skill coupled with care is the trademark here.

Disruption in the hallway

Secondary schools, and to a lesser extent middle schools, can be like transport terminals, with the hustle and bustle of people moving in different directions as students relocate from one classroom to another. Often students are talkative and vocal during this transition time. What should a teacher do if a group of older students are gathered outside the classroom, talking loudly and uninhibitedly while the teacher is taking a class?

The most effective strategy is the most obvious one: talk with them about the disruptive nature of their conversations:

Teacher: Okay guys, listen up. We are in the middle of a lesson in here, and your talking is very distracting. I appreciate that you have a lot to say at this time so could you carry on the conversation in the student common room or during your break. Thanks guys.

Dispense the directive firmly, then turn away and go back into the room with the expectation that the students will move on. The key to this strategy is to approach the students in a nonthreatening way, by using gestures and a warm (rather than stern) facial expression. Older students may be more challenging, but they are also more likely to co-operate if they can own their own decision. One or two of the group might make a cheeky comment, but this is better tactically ignored. Admonishing and berating the students might work for younger students (or it might not), but it may be problematic for older ones. Avoid confrontations. Be firm, be brief, be gone.

Summary

A major determinant within the learning environment is effective communication, based on teacher and student relationships. In order to enhance relationships, teachers must not dismiss their managerial responsibilities at the expense of their instructional responsibilities; each is reliant on the other. A disciplined and orderly environment enables teaching and learning to be facilitated with minimum fuss, which in turn inspires confidence and enjoyment for all.

However, because classrooms are characterised by markers such as multidimensionality, simultaneity, immediacy, unpredictability, publicness, and history, teachers require sets of skills that will help them deal with the mild to moderate forms of challenging behaviour which are the most prevalent enemies of quality instructional time. Such skills are able to be developed by teachers in various ways, experience being but one of these. In addition to experience, practice can be informed by research. Just as Wheldall and Merrett, Kounin, and Jones drew from practice to inform their research, teachers can draw from the research to inform their own practice.

Some of the theories and models most widely recognised as useful have been briefly outlined in this chapter. The early scholars of discipline should be applauded for what they offer in terms of promoting student learning and managing classroom behaviours. The works by noted scholars in the field help us to map the relationships between research and practice, and the kinds of understandings and behaviours (cognitive, ethical, practical, and social) that teachers need to acquire in the course of their experiences and interactions in classrooms and schools.

A slight variation occurs in the final section of this chapter as the emphasis moves toward a range of scenarios that are introduced and explained. The detailed descriptions and meanings inherent in these scenarios offer examples of teachers who are successful in establishing control through democratic processes. The scenarios exemplify some of the practices-in-action that are recognised as being significant in managing behaviour difficulties. Some situations will be more demanding or less demanding than others, and one must always accept that some teachers will be able to develop intervention strategies with students in ways other than those described here.

CHAPTER 5

Students on track at Railway School:
strategies for dealing with severe behaviour difficulties

Introduction

Strategies designed to prevent misbehaviour are the natural starting point, and they matter immensely. However, although generic classroom management efforts are sufficient for most students, there will always be some students who require more intensive and specialised support (Meyer & Evans, 2006; Sugai, 2004). Secondary (or targeted) interventions are appropriate for those individuals who have difficulty responding to generic classroom interventions, and/or whose behaviour is moving toward the severe side of the continuum (see Table 3.1). When this occurs, teachers need to take action (discipline) that is aimed specifically at addressing the more severe or serious challenges to the classroom environment.

It appears that in recent decades, the threat of hostile and aggressive behaviour has increased at a frightening rate. Teachers feel abused and disrespected. Student exposure to drugs and bullying is commonplace. Buildings and equipment are regular targets for tagging—even vandalism. The cost to society is alarming. Gray and Richer (1992) propose that it is possible to sketch a profile of those students who are most likely to be involved in disruptive behaviours:

They are likely to be boys of below average ability, from disharmonious homes where their relationships with their parents are unsettled. At school they see themselves as being of low academic ability, and as getting on badly with staff. They are widely disliked by their peers, and are blamed by the teachers for the disruptive incidents they are involved in, while they themselves see the fault lying with the teachers and the school. (p. 7)

Many of the students that fit the Gray and Richer (1992) profile are amongst the growing number of students considered to be at risk. Schools are often in a quandary about what to do with these students. They search for answers to questions such as: "What is the situation? Have we exhausted our economical and human resources? Are our techniques, processes, and procedures working in favour of students who are presenting with serious challenges? Should we be exploring alternative options?"

This line of questioning will yield two possible answers that can lead to effective outcomes: first, "we have not yet exhausted all of the possibilities open to us and we will continue to make the best possible provision for this student in our school"; and secondly, "a comprehensive alternative programme (that provides enriching experiences through a meaningful curriculum) will be the best option for this student". Both answers are realistic, provided that each genuinely has the best interests of the individual at heart. According to Edmonds (1979, p. 23), "We can, whenever and wherever we choose, successfully teach all children whose schooling is of interest to us."

The first part of this chapter, Lessons from Railway School, reports on a small study of a special school in New Zealand that has effectively catered for students with severe behaviour difficulties (Macfarlane, 2003). The second part, Responding to severe behaviour difficulties, offers a range of strategies and pathways for teachers and administrators to consider in terms of the extreme or severe behaviour difficulties that can pose major problems for schools.

Lessons from Railway School

The school that is here referred to as Railway School provided programmes that met the educational and social needs of students similar to those in the profile sketched by Gray and Richer (1992), except for one important detail: most of the students who attended Railway School were Māori, thus reinforcing the global concern that students from ethnic minority backgrounds are more likely to be disproportionately placed in special education programmes and classes.

Railway School was opened in 1986 as an official Department of Education Activity Centre. These centres are for secondary school students experiencing severe difficulties within the regular school system. The centres are operationally funded by the Ministry of Education. At Railway School, as at other centres, a management committee set the day-to-day running policies, including enrolment, and was legally responsible to the board of trustees of a local secondary school. The main reasons for referring students for enrolment at Railway School were for behaviours described as aggressive or defiant toward teachers and/or students. Truancy and substance abuse were also commonly associated with these students' activities. Students were referred mainly by five secondary schools in the city, and sometimes by secondary schools in the provinces. The recommended tenure of a student at Railway School at that time was a minimum of one school term (then, approximately 13 weeks), and a maximum of one year. The aim was for the student to be successfully reintegrated into the regular school and classroom environment after that time.

Railway School was identified as modelling good practice in the management of behaviours of disaffected adolescents. Some of the key factors that contributed to the success of the programme at the school are reported here. These factors were later developed into the Hikairo Rationale (Macfarlane, 1997, 2004), which is outlined in Chapter 7.

The research participants included 19 students who were attending Railway School at the time of the study, 41 former students, and 33 significant adults. Māori students who had been excluded from the mainstream accounted for 90 percent of enrolments over the 10-year life of the school (Kelly, 1990; Macfarlane, 2003). All enrolled students were asked to respond to a questionnaire about personal esteem, interpersonal relationships, school programmes, and comparisons of the Railway context with that of their former schools. All former students who could be located were also asked to respond to a similar questionnaire.

Adult participants were selected on the basis of significant interactions with the students and the programmes. These included former teachers and support staff, private education providers, social workers, health workers, transition co-ordinators, polytechnic course co-ordinators, secondary school guidance counsellors, and parents of former students.

The research focused on progress made by students over periods ranging from one term (for currently enrolled students) to four years (for former students). For former students, this four-year period included their time back at their base school, and/or their time after they had left school. Several case descriptions were undertaken to exemplify the changes that had taken place in the young person's life, and to show how change was able to be attributed to the school programme. The cases endeavoured to illustrate the impact that whanaungatanga (relationship building) and manaakitanga (the ethic of caring) had on the learning process and on student behaviour, and whether the concept of collective responsibility (student, whānau, school) was a significant factor in the programme.

The effectiveness of the programme was examined, with particular emphasis on the valuing of learning, and the building of relationships. Because of the consistently large number of Māori enrolments, there was an assumption that the learning activities and routines within the programme would largely be Māori in nature, and would therefore support and validate Māori values, a challenge posed by Spoonley (1988) and later by Bevan-Brown (2006) to the state education system. The results later verified that assumption.

The regular curriculum

The morning programme at Railway School had an academic focus. The day always began with a hui (assembly) where the daily programme was outlined in detail. The hui set the scene. Students were clear about the order of activities for the ensuing six hours. Language studies was the first period, prior to interval, followed by mathematics and modular studies (social sciences or natural sciences). Students worked in small groups or individually, and appeared comfortable with the routines that were in place. Staff were actively engaged and interactive throughout.

A karakia (prayer) recited by all preceded a shared lunch. After the lunch break came a 15–20 minute period of individual reading. Students then changed into sports gear for an hour of physical activity, encouraging teamwork and fitness. Other options during this time were cultural activities such as maurākau (long staff drills), haka (dances with chant), and waiata (songs). A brief hui brought the school day to a close.

This balanced programme acknowledged the formal curriculum, which included the social, cultural, emotional, and academic needs of the students. The programme showed evidence of both pastoral care and the attainment of functional academic skills. Rutter et al. (1979) report that teachers who concentrate on the lesson topic, who sometimes make the class work silently (noise level zero), and who start and finish their lessons on time, encourage better behaviour from their students than teachers who do not. Rutter and his colleagues suggest that children tend to make better progress, both behaviourally and academically, when an appropriate emphasis is placed on academic matters.

The timetable at Railway School provided for such a balance. The instructional planning by staff encompassed assessment, learning prescriptions, and evaluations for each student or group of students. Knowledge of each student's abilities, interests, skill development, and learning styles was essential to the assessment processes. Student groupings for learning ranged from individuals and small groups to the whole school, depending on the learning situation or the topic.

The regular curriculum followed a set of proactive approaches that were platformed on the building of positive relationships, having a set of routines, and the implementation of appropriate behaviour strategies. In essence, positive relationships set the stage for learning to occur. The routines provided predictability and consistency. The strategies that teachers employed drew from many of those outlined in the literature (Charles, 1999, 2002; Wearmouth et al., 2005; Wheldall & Merrett, 1989) and described in Chapter 4, with importance given to implementing these with a balance of assertiveness and integrity. In many instances teachers had to teach replacement behaviours.

The hidden curriculum

The hidden curriculum was able to be manifested in more subtle ways. Preedy (1989) has claimed that, although not part of the formal intention of schooling, the hidden curriculum has a particularly powerful and lasting impact on most children. Since children spend a great deal of their time in school, the ethos or climate of the school is an important influence. Eisner (1994) argues that what schools do *not* teach may be as important as what they *do* teach. Many of the human qualities of the hidden curriculum are not prescribed or mandated. Teachers, students, and peers of the school comprise the human elements of the school's ecosystem.

At Railway School, this ecosystem was deliberately fashioned in terms of what Goodlad (1997, p. 110) calls the "human connection", and Graham Smith (1995, p. 32) refers to as "the notion of whānau as a core feature of kaupapa Māori theory". Each of these propositions encapsulates the condition where all of those closely connected to the school come together to create a particular wairua or school spirit, in a simple yet powerful way. Goodlad (1997) contends that schools should also be enjoyable and popular settings, with no need to radically disturb the educative and humanistic mix.

Creating this ethos is often made possible by attention to the subtle effects of the setting in which the formal education occurs—the unstated rules necessary for successful completion of the formal part of studies. At Railway School, as in many other schools, students were encouraged to acquire social norms and values that the school promoted. These norms and values include habits such as punctuality, patience, common sense, and initiative.

Railway School's environment was conducive to the hidden curriculum impacting positively on at-risk youth. Teachers and staff were expected to be role models *par excellence*. Their appearance, mannerisms, tone of voice, sincerity, gentleness, and firmness were the qualities employed to help instil in the students respect for moral values, and tolerance and appreciation of themselves and others.

A cultural presence

In addition to the regular and hidden curricula, the school's design and construction reflected genuine bicultural perspectives. A tukutuku (ornamental lattice work) panel featured on one wall. This design featured a marae as the heart of the community. It was woven by students during a three-day noho marae (live-in experience in a traditional Māori setting). A small plaque dedicated the tukutuku work to the memory of a kuia (an elderly Māori woman) who had played a leading role in the cultural activities of the school. Instructional stations, a library corner, and a multipurpose work area were strategically placed. Students' work was displayed in innovative ways.

Railway School adopted the practice of a three-day marae visit as part of the Term One calendar. While attendance for the noho marae was not compulsory, the records showed that there were no refusers. The marae experience focused on the values of aroha (acceptance), manaakitanga (caring), and kotahitanga (unity). The rationale was to infuse and embed those values into the students' lives when they returned to school and home. Again, the study provided evidence that the marae experience was significant in focusing students on the expectation that they behave responsibly, across contexts.

A study of Alternative Education Centres, commissioned by the Ministry of Māori Development (Clark et al., 1996), revealed some inconsistencies and variabilities in the Māori component of alternative education programmes, in that the needs differed widely across different environments. The schools they studied articulated very clearly the philosophies that underpinned their programmes; these tended to be based on improving the behaviour of individual students, and empowering them to take more responsibility for their own actions. However, in some instances the researchers found that although the emphases on taha Māori (Māori aspects) came through the curriculum, they were not actually embedded in the classroom ethos or culture. The majority of these schools did not appear to accord Māoritanga a high priority in practice.

Railway School was a notable exception. The programmes were staffed by qualified Māori and non-Māori who had an interest in and knowledge of behavioural principles and adolescent development as well as Māori ecologies. This expertise, coupled with the regular input from other agencies competent in Māori and bicultural knowledge, enhanced the school's ability to put cultural values and tikanga (customs) into practice.

Voices of the students

Students have often been described as being the most discerning consumers of education. When asked to comment on their school experiences, students are often open, willing to respond, confident about their thoughts, and articulate (see also Bishop & Berryman, 2006; Cookson-Cox, 2006). The students in the Railway School study were open, willing, and articulate. Many of them were giving similar messages in many instances, and using very direct language. Table 5.1 is a small sample taken from in excess of 100 responses to a questionnaire from 41 former students. The students were asked to draw comparisons between and comment on staff and programmes at Railway School and their base (referring) school.

Forty out of the 41 former Railway School students took the opportunity to make further comments of their own. All these students commented favourably on the staff and programmes at Railway School. There was not a single negative voice. However, the comments made about the staff and programmes at their other secondary schools were openly critical of both style and method. While the responses from the enrolled cohort are not included here, these correlated strongly with the responses of their older counterparts.

The programme at Railway School dispelled some of the myths that have evolved in relation to at-risk students, and have become barriers to successful efforts to help them. These students do not need easy work. Like all other students, they need to be academically challenged. Regular classroom teachers on their own cannot adequately address the needs of at-risk students.

Table 5.1 Students' comments on staff and programmes

Your thoughts about staff at Railway School	Your thoughts about staff at the base school	Your thoughts about the programme at Railway School
Easy to get along with, fun. Very interactive with students—friendly, open, kind, and helpful.	Couldn't talk to them. Too pushy. Just worried about doing their job.	They were very exciting and educational. The programmes were also sporting and physically helpful.
The staff at Railway were very kind, helpful, and big-hearted. They helped me a lot.	The staff at my other school were everything that I couldn't stand. They made me turn off school.	Programmes at Railway helped me to get my self-esteem and confidence back. I felt that the programmes were at a level where everybody could understand and weren't confused.
Good! One thing about Railway is that we were never treated like children. Teachers could be hard, but fair. They keep you on track all the time.	Most of the staff only had time for students with high grades and that were little angels. The staff didn't really take time for the students who really needed help.	Tumeke bro!! (colloquialism for "terrific" my friend).
They were choice and they never made me feel unwelcome. I really enjoyed their company.	They were alright but not as good as the Railway teachers.	Really choice, really exciting, and really fun to do.
I reckon they were and still are cool. They are kind, understanding, and intelligent people.	They don't take time to listen to any of the students. At least at Railway they had time for all students.	I reckon they were quite cool—it helped me a lot. Thank you.
The staff at Railway School were always there to talk to. They made us work hard but it was clear what we had to do. They were and still are friendly and caring.	From what I remember the teachers were too worried about how we looked coming into class. I never learned much from the teaching that took place at the school.	Really top programmes. They helped me a lot. I got to know myself and others. I've learned things that I've never known. I think every school should have programmes like this. With this programme more teenagers would stay at school, they would find it more interesting.

Classroom teachers can contribute, but addressing the needs of at-risk students requires a team effort. Railway School was adamant that its curricula were based on improving academic performance, as well as modifying behaviour, and it constantly challenged students to raise the bar. The staff placed emphasis on working as a team, and implemented a model involving in-school organisation, home and school associations, and accountability in relation to a set of educational standards and goals. The programme at Railway School was widely acknowledged, and this letter from a parent is humble testament to that:

Figure 5.1 Letter from a parent about her child, Ricky (pseudonym)

> To whom it may concern
>
> My son Ricky is an ex-student of Railway School from [previous school]. Ricky attended Railway in [year] until the end of [year] where he left at the age of 16 years. He was having a lot of behaviour problems as well as learning problems at [previous school]. I have nothing but the highest recommendation for the head teacher and his team at Railway. Since Ricky attended Railway, his attitude towards school changed and so did his attendance. He started doing well in subjects where he was at the bottom at [previous school]. His school reports changed to very good–average instead of poor. He came home with numerous certificates from courses and studies [head teacher] and his team held. Finally a great surprise towards the end of the year when Ricky passed his Form 5 awards in English and Maths. Ricky now has a C.V. that any parent would be proud of.
>
> I owe all our thanks and am very grateful to the high standards of [head teacher] and the team at Railway. Ricky is now 18 years old and has a full time job drain-laying so instead of becoming a drop out, which I was sure he was heading at [previous school]. Thanks [head teacher] for turning my son's life around. I wish you all the best in the future.
>
> [Mother]

Staff-related issues

Fraser (cited in Fraser et al., 1995) contends that the effective teacher is both caring and firm, genuine and assertive, empathetic and honest. General themes to emerge regarding the staff at Railway School included friendliness, helpfulness, encouragement, understanding, communicativeness, fairness, supportiveness, openness, kindness, and the concept of whānau. Staff at the other schools were criticised for their lack of empathy, prejudice, lack of communication, and lack of understanding of the specific needs of the students. The Railway School programmes were considered to contain elements such as enjoyment, planning which catered for individual needs, excitement, challenges, and confidence building.

Three specific themes emerged from the study. These included issues relating to the individual, issues relating to relationships, and issues relating to learning:

The individual

- Students want respect for who they are.
- Students long for achieving a sense of self-esteem and confidence.
- Students know their vulnerabilities and appreciate fair discipline procedures.

Relationships

- Secondary students have not outgrown the need for care and kindness.
- Students prefer adults who take time to get to know them.
- Students prefer teachers who state clear directions, and who are firm.

Learning

- Students learn at different rates and levels.
- If challenged, students will respond, given necessary and appropriate support.
- Good teachers are valued.

At Railway School, students felt included and safe. They began to experience success in the programmes that the school provided, and reciprocated the personal value that was extended to them. They did not have to feel circumspect about themselves because they were keenly invited into the academic and social activities that were on offer. This involvement meant that they could convert apathy and noncommitance—characteristics related to the concept of whakamā, into motivation and willingness—characteristics related to the concept of mana. A school spirit based on accomplishment and communication helped to reinstate personal conviction and self-esteem.

Linking practice and theory

At Railway School, as at other schools and classrooms that focus on outcomes for students, the realisation of formal and informal education was determined in multiple ways.

The programme at Railway School provides an excellent example of the links that are able to be made between practice and theory. Many of the students were experiencing inner turmoil and personality tensions. These students often required interventions from the psychodynamic model, such as counselling and life-space interviews. Some students were described as hyperactive, while others were withdrawn. In such cases they required monitoring linked to the biophysical model. Behaviour-theory interventions were regularly invoked by way of reinforcement and shaping processes.

The ecological model and the sociocultural model were both significant in terms of influencing the teaching and learning practices at Railway School. In terms of the ecological model, many of the factors known to influence learning outcomes, such as environmental influences and the instructional techniques, were consciously attended to. In terms of the sociocultural model, insightfulness regarding cultural meanings and a sound knowledge of the backgrounds of the students were critical.

Responding to severe behaviour difficulties

Notwithstanding the reasonable level of success for the students at Railway School, one must not lose sight of the fact that they were referred to the programme because they presented with severe behaviour difficulties. The teachers in the programme had to have some understanding of behaviour principles, as well as a repertoire of strategies to respond positively and appropriately. More than ever before, teachers, resource teachers, parents, and advocates are becoming aware of the need to deal with severe behaviour difficulties in a way that is less intrusive and more dignified. Teachers seek ideas for responding to aggressive and abusive behaviours, such as high-level swearing, put-downs, and bullying, and also to truancy. Some ideas for dealing effectively with these behaviours follow.

As was the case in the previous chapter, the tone and style of the writing will now alter to accommodate some practical orientations for responding to the more severe behaviour difficulties that are manifested in classrooms and schools. Again, the work of Rogers (1995), and Wright (1998), as well as the work of Cookson-Cox (2006), Dunckley (2005), Bateman (2007), and other noted contributors, is acknowledged.

High-level swearing

A student is messing around in a metalwork class and is taking silly risks with an electric drill. The teacher reprimands him for his behaviour and he tells the teacher to "Get f----d!" It is important that this behaviour is dealt with assertively, so that the students know it is not going to be tolerated. The student is exhibiting a combination of defiance and verbal aggression, and must be told what is wrong about what he is doing:

> Teacher: Craig, I do not talk to you in that way and so I do not expect to be talked to in that way.

This requires the teacher to discuss with Craig (on his own) the reason for the outburst, and to look for a way to apologise or make amends. Talking to Craig calmly about the school rule on swearing and how to behave next time is also necessary. This is a form of life-space interview, also referred to as "emotional first aid on the spot" (Walker & Shea, 1999). The purpose of this strategy is to assist the student through a rough situation so that they are able to continue an activity, and remain within the rules and boundaries of the class. This strategy, when tactfully introduced by the teacher, can reduce the student's frustration levels and support him or her through an emotionally charged situation. The aim is to restore respectful teacher–student communications.

The student may resist the emotional first aid that is applied, therefore some alternatives may be necessary. One alternative is to remove the student from the group, but with an adult (teacher, teacher aide) present to provide contact and support. Reasoning and discussing with the student should not be attempted until the student has regained self-control. Part of the process of regaining self-control might be that the student needs time alone. The teacher needs to respect this wish, while remaining in proximity in case further interaction is necessary.

Finally, consider introducing another phase of the life-space interview—helping the student to generate alternative methods of coping and behaving. The teacher who responds authoritatively and sets a strategy to help the student regain self-control is better poised when it comes to preventing any recurrences.

Put-downs

Put-downs are a form of bullying and are a pervasive problem in schools. For those who are targets of put-downs, the incidents can be painful and lasting. Students should not have to endure being put down by their peers. Teachers need to send a strong message that this type of behaviour is not tolerated. Addressing this behaviour at an early point is critical. Not checking this situation might encourage it to spread, so that more students become engaged in similar behaviour.

Many students might be reluctant to tell teachers that they are being victimised in this way, so teachers need to be alert for signs. Some of these signs include withdrawal from peer interaction, difficulty in focusing on class work and responsibilities, increased anxiety, avoidance of some common areas such as the playground, and resistance to attending school. Therefore, teachers need to prepare responses for both the victim and the perpetrator.

The student being abused needs to be aware that there are some ready responses that they can invoke. One such response includes looking the offending student in the eye, making a confident statement such as "I absolutely dislike the way that you are behaving toward me. It is just not on and I will not tolerate any more of it", then walking away without engaging in the conversation. Another response is to not respond—say nothing at all and walk away. Other strategies include getting the offended student to establish friendships with peers who are kind, understanding, and are often seen as leaders. Teachers should also look for ways of highlighting the offended student's strengths in the presence of classmates, so that he or she is seen in a new light.

Students who put down others are cunning, and they will do so when the teacher is not around. Therefore, it is important to alert other staff and other people (such as the bus driver) to keep a watchful eye and to intervene if necessary.

There are many suggestions in the literature with regard to dealing with the offending student. The following strategy is the foundation on which subsequent interventions are built. It also seems to be a simple and very effective approach that may address the problem to a marked if not complete degree: Talk to the student offender in private. Explain to this student the hurt that is being inflicted, and get the student to consider the feelings that might be experienced if the boot was on the other foot. Ask the student if he or she is upset about something—these students often are. Insist that this behaviour be discontinued immediately.

Bullying

Bullying is deliberate and hurtful, is repeated over a period of time, and is usually difficult for those being bullied to defend themselves against. The three main types of bullying are physical (hitting, kicking, taking belongings), verbal (name-calling, insulting, often involving racist and/or sexist remarks), and indirect (spreading nasty stories, excluding from the group).

A bully is a person who behaves in a way that might meet a need for excitement, material gain, or group process. He or she does not recognise or meet the needs and rights of the other people who are harmed by the behaviour. A victim is a person or group that is harmed by the behaviour of others. He or she does not have the resources, status, or ability to counteract or stop the harmful behaviour.

Responses to bullying can come from schools and students. If there is a problem, schools must acknowledge it and set about raising awareness of the problem. Schools should encourage students and parents to report bullying, discuss bullying in the curriculum, and deal with the problem areas and times. Selected students should be encouraged to undertake assertiveness training and collaborative conflict resolution courses.

Bullying, the silent epidemic, exists in schools throughout the world. Because bullying comes in many forms, it is useful to identify some of the specific types of bullying and to examine how these may be dealt with within classrooms and school environments. Sexual harassment and ethnic harassment in schools are prevalent worldwide. Grossman (2004) refers to these types of bullying as nonphysical forms of aggression—for example being subjected to offensive comments, jokes, and gestures: receiving unwanted sexual or racial messages; having graffiti spread on walls and fences; being called "gay" or "lesbian", or "ching". These are more common than physical forms of bullying, but more often than not, less endurable.

A great deal of research has been done on bullying and its victims and bullying has been at the centre of immense media interest. Smith and Morita (1999) contend that the combination of knowledge-based and resource-funded interventions can reduce levels of bullying, and improve the lives of many students. However, Grossman (2004) is concerned that most schools do not have proactive programmes aimed at reducing bullying but rely on reactive approaches. Consequently, he encourages proactive, comprehensive school-wide approaches that include: promoting a climate that may discourage bullying; establishing school-wide policies; training teachers to change the underlying problems; providing information to students and role-playing intervention strategies; holding classroom meetings; and teaching victims the skills they need to defend themselves against bullies.

The following approach, the NO-BLAME approach to bullying, can be seen as an endeavour in the right direction; one that is aimed at addressing many of the concerns expressed by Grossman (2004), Smith & Moreta (1999), and indeed many others.

The NO-BLAME approach to bullying

Following attendance at a professional development seminar promoted by the New Zealand Police in 1998, Sonja Bateman introduced the NO-BLAME approach in the school she was teaching in at that time. This approach to bullying is being adopted in a number of schools in New Zealand and other countries. Essentially it looks to identify how the victim is being affected by the bullying, and then uses a support group made up of peers, colluders, and perpetrators. By not blaming or punishing anyone, the group itself is encouraged to take responsibility for the problem and deal with it. An outline of the NO-BLAME approach follows.

At the point where the school acknowledges that the problem of bullying exists, it must set out to:
- raise awareness
- talk about it ... "We don't accept bullying here" etc.
- encourage children to report any bullying
- be receptive to any reporting of bullying
- remember that the victim *cannot* deal with, or stop, the bullying behaviour: the bully / bullies must change *their* behaviour
- involve the silent majority—the bystanders and colluders
- introduce staff to the Bully sociograph (Figure 5.1).

Teacher receives a report of bullying from a victim

STEP ONE
- Talk to the victim: provide empathy and support.
- Praise the victim for coming forward.
- Tell the victim that you will help sort it out.
- Ask the victim to identify:

  This becomes the CONFERENCE
  - the bullies—the two or three main ones
  - the bystanders and colluders—two or three students with whom they are comfortable in their class; they may have been friends with these students previously
  - the leaders (bully-proof students)—two or three students they admire; they may be in another class.

STEP TWO
- Ask the victim to write down how they feel about being bullied—what the bullying does to them, their feelings ... (encourage them to really "let it out" on paper). You may need to scribe for them as they talk.

Figure 5.2 Bully sociograph

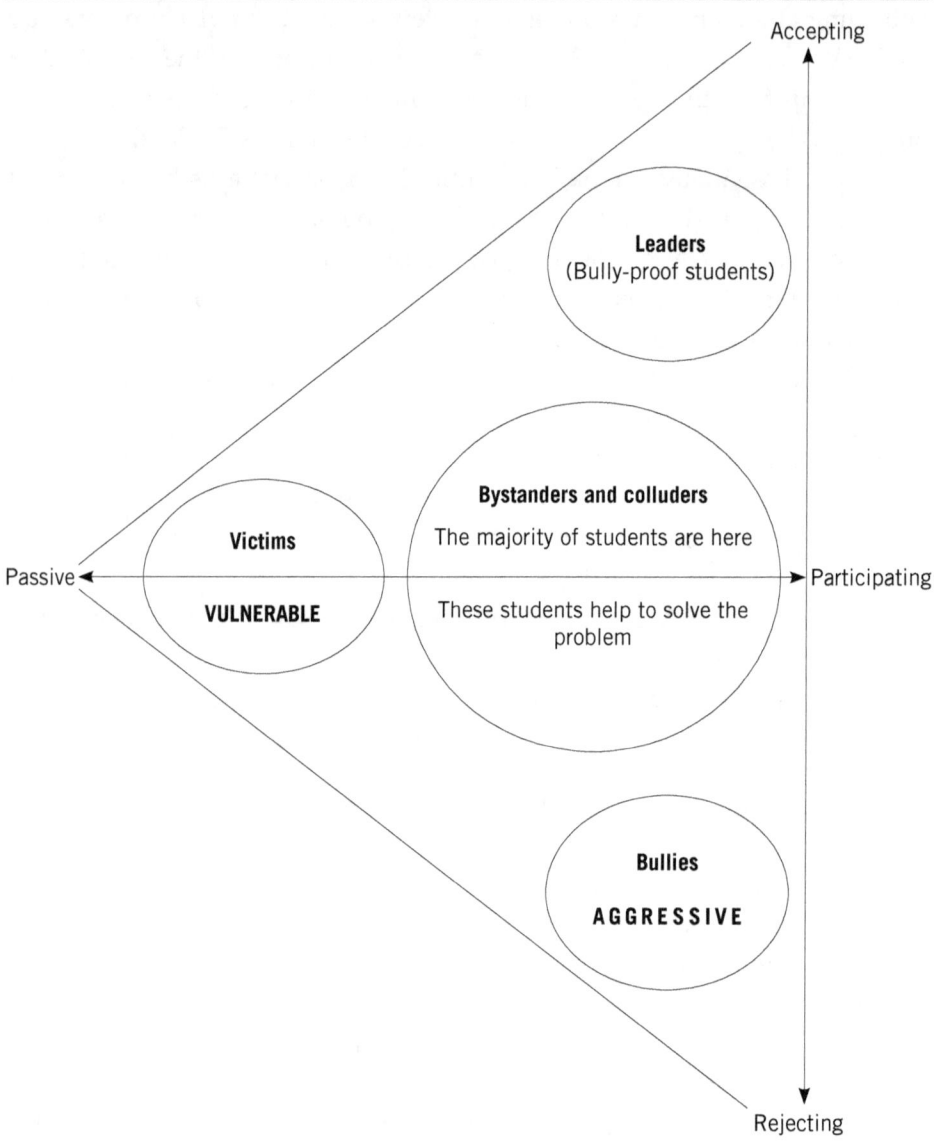

- Ask if you can use the letter at the conference you are going to have, to sort things out.

Note: The victim does not attend the conference.

STEP THREE

The conference:
- Inform the students (previously chosen by the victim) that they are to attend a conference to help sort out a bullying problem. Over lunch is a great time to hold the conference.
- At the conference, state: "We are here for a reason—we have a problem with bullying—and we are all going to help sort it out …"
- Mention: "This is a NO-BLAME conference—we are not here to go over whose fault it is, who started it, or who did what … we are going to resolve the problem."
- Read out the letter written by the victim. (Do not name the victim at this point.)
- Draw a simple version of the sociograph to describe what bullying looks like; what the dynamics of bullying situations are. Provide a general description of the characteristics of each of the four groups (bullies, leaders, bystanders/colluders, and victims).
- Inform the group who the victim is.
- Explain that the victim has identified them individually as a key person—and so you (the teacher) believe that they would make an excellent group member to help solve the problem. (Do not place the students into any of these groups—the bullies will most likely realise where they reside!)
- Then initiate some problem solving. Make statements like: "This can't go on, can it?", "How can we all help?", and "Each student needs to offer at least one idea to help sort this out and make things better for _____."

Some ideas are likely to be:
- "I could sit with him/her at lunchtime."
- "I could walk home with him/her."
- "I could ask him/her to join in our game."
- "If I see anyone name-calling or bullying him/her, I'll go and help, or get a teacher."

- Go over *all* suggestions again. Often the bullies may not offer anything, so ask them directly what they can do to help the situation.
- Set up a follow-up conference for one week away to monitor and review progress.
- Continue to support the victim.
- Send a letter home to *all* conference members' families to praise the positive contribution that their son or daughter is making to the school through attending this support group.

Truancy

Participating in education is basic to student achievement. In New Zealand, the Education Act 1999 requires that parents enrol their children at a school and that they attend. Why do students truant? A study commissioned by the Rotorua District Council Truancy Action Group and prepared for publication by Candy Cookson-Cox (2006, p. 5) draws from the voices of the truanting students themselves:

> I want to go to another school but my mother won't let me, so that's why I wag (male, 14 years).
>
> My mother works a lot and I'm always home on my own, no one really encourages me to go to school (male, 15 years).
>
> I don't like the teachers at my school, particularly one teacher because she lies (female, 15 years).
>
> The school work sucks and the teachers are boring. The work is not appropriate; I get into trouble for no reason (male, 14 years).
>
> When friends want to wag I just wag and go along with them (female, 15 years).
>
> The reason why I wagged school was to go to the shops, till I ended up being expelled with a drug issue (female, 15 years).
>
> I didn't like the teachers. They were always picking on me. My dad is in jail and that contributed to my [lack of] attendance. I was also being bullied by other girls (female, 14 years).
>
> Play Station was more important to me. The style of teaching [at school] was not suited to me. I'm more a hands on learner (male, 17 years).
>
> Because I wanted to do something different, then it became a habit (female, 16 years).
>
> When my friends wagged I wagged also, because if I never I'd be on my own (female, 16 years).

Cookson-Cox (2006) identified four broad zones of influence as having a significant effect on the behaviour of young people who engage in truancy: school; teachers; friends; and home and/or parents. Under another category, "other", further important issues were identified. Table 5.2 summarises some important perspectives on truancy that emerged in the Rotorua District Council study.

Table 5.2 A perspective on truancy (with acknowledgement to Cookson-Cox, 2006)

Main category	Drivers of truancy	Identified solutions
School	Lack of practical, activity-based learning Lack of a suitable range of courses on offer Bullying	Development of appropriate programmes of learning Offering a broader range of vocational- or trade-related subjects Monitoring and dealing with bullying
Teachers	Teaching styles Relationship building and communication	Teachers demonstrate more enthusiasm, care, creativity, and interest in lessons Instructional match Model acceptable behaviour Pay attention to building relationships Offer opportunities to engage in professional development around strategies for dealing with (difficult) students
Friends	Peer pressure The development of a social circle of truanting Promoting an image of "cool", which includes shop lifting and smoking	Full-time counsellors on site Having a cultural committee to advise students Creating a mentoring peer support system Self-esteem building and recognition for personal achievements
Home	Parental guidance and influence	More research and thought needs to be invested, given the complexities relating to this area
Other	General health of the student Transferring schools and transferring years Better designed policies and procedures around truancy	Access to food, adequate sleep, a safe environment, regular transport, correct school uniform Second-hand clothing stock for students requiring this form of assistance Cheaper canteen prices Access to full-time school counsellor

While truancy is a serious matter, it should be noted that the vast majority of students attend school. A Ministry of Education survey carried out in 2004 found that the participating schools had an overall truancy rate of 3.4 percent over one week in 2004. Secondary schools had the highest truancy rate. The Ministry of Education is continuing to put effort into reducing truancy. The

Government has introduced a Student Engagement Initiative (SEI), supports District Truancy Services (DTS), and administers the Suspension Reduction Initiative (SRI). However, the major responsibility for addressing truancy issues lies with schools (Ministry of Education, 2004).

Options of last resort

Teachers in New Zealand are not permitted to hit, cane, or in any way physically punish the students in their care. Boards of trustees may approve other means of discipline, aversive and nonaversive, and schools may consider referring students for participation in special programmes. Some examples of aversive means of discipline include time-out, withdrawal of privileges, setting extra homework, or keeping a student in after school (detention). If the behaviour is more serious, students may be stood down or suspended from a school for a period of time or, if over the age of 16, excluded (not allowed to return). In the case of suspension or exclusion, formal procedures apply. The use of physical restraint must be used only as a last resort, when and where it is necessary to ensure people are safe. Group Special Education (GSE) offices have staff with knowledge and expertise in this area.

Time-out

Time-out is a form of punishment that involves students being removed from a location for infraction of rules. In time-out, students are removed from a situation where they would usually expect reinforcement and are placed in a situation where they cannot be reinforced. If students like to be in class, being removed may be interpreted as a punitive measure. Therefore, the effectiveness of time-out is somewhat reliant on the quality of the time-in.

There are different forms of time-out: "exclusionary time-out", "inclusionary time-out", and "easy change" (Dunckley, 2005). A common exclusionary time-out procedure might require a student to sit at the back of the room, facing in the opposite direction, where he or she cannot observe or participate in an activity for a set period. This strategy involves removal of the student from the activity, but not the environment. Inclusionary time-out, also known as "mini time-out", is a planned procedure where a student self-initiates their removal to a specified space in the classroom for a brief period of time, usually less than a minute. According to Dunckley (2005):

> ... Students themselves choose to use mini time-out. The motivation for students to use mini time-out is that it gives them the opportunity to shift out of a developing

situation with minimal fuss and then be able to return to the group within a short period of time and without a more severe consequence being implemented. Mini time-out needs to be implemented in the early stages of uncooperative behaviour, before students become aggressive. It is more effective when it has been planned, discussed and practised with the student prior to a demand being made. With prior discussion and planning, students know what to do and they also know that there will be no more serious consequences. (pp. 29–30)

Easy change is also a planned procedure that involves the student being motivated to walk from a room to engage in an alternative activity. The alternative, previously practised, activity has the potential to calm the student so that the return to class is relatively quick and flurry-free. Engagement in some ball routines or jogging are examples of alternative activities. Because students see themselves as having some ownership of the decision making, and know that re-entry to the classroom will be a routine passage, easy change has a good compliance rating. This strategy teaches self-control under difficult conditions, and all the while the teacher remains in charge of the situation.

Stand-down, suspension, exclusion, and expulsion

According to Conway (cited in Ashman & Elkins, 2002), students exhibiting severe misbehaviours are among the first to be referred out of or ejected from regular classes, and are among the last to be socially reintegrated back into them. These exclusionary options should be a last rather than a first resort.

The Ministry of Education's *Education Circular 1999/06* (1999) outlines what is meant by a stand-down, suspension, exclusion, and expulsion. Stand-down means the formal removal of a student from school for a specified period. Stand-downs of a particular student can total no more than five school days in a term or ten school days in a year. Suspension means the formal removal of a student from school until the board of trustees decides the outcome at a suspension meeting. Exclusion means the formal removal of a student aged under 16 from the school and the requirement that the student enrol elsewhere. Expulsion means the formal removal of a student, aged 16 or over, from the school, and if the student wishes to continue schooling, he or she may enrol elsewhere. Exclusion and expulsion are for the most serious cases only.

It is recommended that these last resort strategies are exactly that—a last resort. The school must reflect on whether it has taken into account what has been done previously, and whether it has done everything that it should, and everything it could.

Special programmes

Many schools also employ nonaversive strategies and special programmes in their search for responses to severe and challenging behaviours that some students persistently exhibit. These forms of intervention require more time and resourcing, but the dividends that accrue make the commitment worthwhile. Restorative conferencing, conflict resolution, antibullying programmes, social skills training, and anger management courses are now widely accepted by schools as passages toward more lasting and effective outcomes. Some of the special programmes available to schools include DARE, Kia Kaha, and the Tū Tangata approach to working with students requiring extra support.

The DARE Foundation's Skills for Life programmes are New Zealand-designed programmes which seek to challenge students, parents, and their communities to DARE to develop skills in decision making, assertiveness, responsibility, and esteem, so as to help them to make informed choices. The programmes are the responsibility of the New Zealand Police and the DARE community. Another New Zealand Police initiative, in conjunction with Youth Education Service (YES), is Kia Kaha, a whole-school approach to eliminate bullying. The programme is designed to respond to enquiries from schools and to assist the Kia Kaha co-ordinator in the school with the implementation of the whole-school approach, as required. The Tū Tangata programme primarily involves placing people from the community in the role of Education Support Personnel (ESP), who work in the classroom alongside the students. Particular students are targeted, and the ESP work specifically with these students, but also provide assistance to other students where needed. ESP are often members of the targeted student's whānau. The Tū Tangata programme is funded and managed by the Ministry of Education to support students at risk of poor educational outcomes.

Summary

Meaningful and well-constructed learning experiences are at the heart of managing student behaviour in classrooms. Classroom management is successfully manifested when conventional strategies are introduced with precision and skill. While there are multiple ideas and considerations for practitioners to draw from, it must be noted that not all students will respond in a way that teachers would hope. When this happens, the responses of the teacher convert from classroom management to discipline. Some students exhibit, for any number of reasons, more severe behaviours. Such students are perceived as a threat to teacher control and contributors to teacher stress. As a consequence, teachers need to get better at responding to behaviours that are aggressive and defiant—behaviours such as high-level swearing, put-downs, bullying, and truancy. Where proactive, nonintrusive, and punitive strategies have been unsuccessful, there are options of last resort.

In this chapter a picture was sketched of students who exhibit severe behaviours. It was shown how a special school was able to successfully respond to the needs of these students. While this might appear to highlight one of the paradoxes of inclusion, it demonstrates that whatever and wherever the setting, fairness and empathy can prevail over ignorance and apathy.

Certainly the students in the Railway School study responded to teachers who demonstrated good classroom management skills and dealt with disciplinary matters skilfully. This study concluded that a number of additional benefits accrued to the school. The programme reduced nonattendance, led to improved student–teacher relationships, provided a proactive framework for the delivery of education to disaffected students, and improved the school's standing in the community.

The Railway School programme also changed students' perceptions of authority. This change was facilitated through contact with people who exercised authority rationally, and who valued what others said or did. Since the Railway School programme was built on basic values of caring for and helping one another, staff members had to be fully committed to the caring process. The students appreciated the caring processes of which they had been part. The assertive yet warm approaches epitomised by Railway School staff helped many of the students to progress their aspirations, to raise their self-esteem, and to steer clear of troublesome situations. The learning and social experiences at Railway School helped to rekindle young people's interest in education and gave them the opportunity to complete their compulsory schooling, either by returning to the mainstream or moving into appropriate tertiary opportunities.

While Railway School was oriented toward promoting the value of respect, this was not a reference to any specific ideology. Rather, there was one basic value—the value of being a human being. The programme design reflected the position of Felsenstein (1987), in that the educational experiences demonstrated to each student that the school—the teachers—value him or her, while also creating opportunities for success. Adults were willing to listen to students in order to help untangle some of their confusion. There was evidence of collective responsibility set within a pedagogically sound and culturally inclusive environment. Such environments are not only safe; they also provide students with a sense of belonging.

A slight variation occurs in the final section of this chapter in terms of linking theory to practice, and in terms of moving the emphases more directly toward what schools can do about some of the more severe behaviours that they encounter. Consequently, a range of intervention strategies and associated school and community programmes are considered. These intervention strategies and programmes are not presented as a dogmatic set of responses that will provide all the answers. Each context is unique, and there are strategies and programmes that are likely to be more fitting and effective within a specific context than those described here. However, focusing on interventions and programmes such as those described here could assist teachers and schools to examine what it is in their programmes that can be improved, or why they are already effective.

PART THREE

LISTENING TO CULTURE

International perspectives on culturally responsive teaching, and the Hikairo Rationale—a culturally responsive approach for working with Māori students and whānau

6 **Culturally responsive teaching:** evidence from classic research studies in the United States and New Zealand

7 **The Hikairo Rationale:** a culturally responsive approach for working with students with behaviour difficulties
  - Huakina mai: opening doorways
  - Ihi: being assertive
  - I runga i te manaaki: growing a caring community
  - Rangatiratanga: motivating learners
  - Kōtahitanga: linking home and school
  - Awhinatia: moving toward restorative practice
  - Orangatanga: developing a nurturing environment

CHAPTER 6

Culturally responsive teaching:
evidence from classic research studies
in the United States and New Zealand

Introduction

One of the most popular themes in contemporary discourses on teaching students with learning and behaviour difficulties is that of the teacher who is not only adept at their craft, but is also empathetic toward the individual status of the students. Franklin (1998) describes these teachers as heroic and valiant teachers:

> Often contrasted with his or her more conventionally minded colleagues, this teacher is depicted as one whose sentiments and attitudes render him or her a champion of the child. Heroic teachers typically are described as those whose affectional qualities manifest themselves in a respect for childhood, a dislike for bureaucratic rules and administrative authority, and an openness to curricular and pedagogical innovation. (p. 28)

Eisner (1994) refers to teaching as an art that is guided by educational values and personal needs. He perceives such teachers (artistes) as having the ability to perform skilfully, to function in innovative ways, and to deal inventively with what occurs in the class. Within their artistic practice, many of the desired outcomes are achieved in the process.

Culturally responsive interventions that benefit all students

Meeting the needs of students from minority cultures, their parents, and the communities within which they live is arguably one of the most overriding priorities, and one that must be framed in terms of equity and best educational practice. Identifying the learning and behaviour needs of minority culture children in a culturally relevant manner also needs to be at the heart of educational philosophies and practices. According to Peer and Reid (2000):

> It is necessary that culture-fair principles and practices are considered in the identification and assessment processes, in classroom practices and provision, the curriculum, in the training of teachers, support assistants and psychologists, in the selection and allocation of resources, in policy and in liaison with parents and the wider community. (p. 1)

The following summaries of studies involving mainly African-American students and their teachers in the United States (USA), and Māori and Pasifika students and their teachers in New Zealand, make it clear that raising awareness and understanding of diversity within the ranks of educational professionals fosters tolerance and proficiency growing at all levels. It is therefore important for educators to foster and support culturally competent teachers, consultants, and organisational systems.

Cultural competence is defined as a set of congruent attitudes, practices, and policies that enable systems, agencies, and professionals to work effectively in crosscultural situations (Cross, Bazron, Dennis, & Isaacs, 1989). A culturally competent system (or programme) and its representatives acknowledge the importance of culture at all levels, incorporating practices that are culturally aware, sensitive, appropriate, and responsive. McIntyre (1996) argues that this requires vigilance in terms of the dynamics that result from cultural differences, the expansion of cultural knowledge, and the adaptation of services to meet culturally unique needs.

The following section discusses several selected studies of some exemplary teachers, many of whom would qualify as Franklin's "heroic" or "valiant" teacher, or Eisner's "artiste". While the teachers in these studies work primarily with students from minority groups, it is argued here that the benefits inherent in their practice would accrue for all students.

The Gloria Ladson-Billings study

Rather than focusing on programmatic reform, a study by Ladson-Billings (1995) prefers to consider educational theorising about teaching practice, and proposes a culturally focused pedagogy that might be considered in the reformation of teacher education. Ladson-Billings suggests that a further necessary step is the development of a theoretical model that not only addresses student achievement, but also helps students to accept and affirm students' cultural identity. A strong cultural identity is necessary for the development of critical perspectives that challenge the inequities which are regularly perpetuated in schools (and other institutions). Ladson-Billings terms this pedagogy, "culturally relevant pedagogy" and takes it to mean, "the kind of teaching that draws on the students' culture to help them achieve success by allowing them to choose academic excellence without losing their sense of personal and cultural identity" (1995, p. 249).

Ladson-Billings (1995) recounts her own work as a lone investigator in 1988 in a small, predominantly African-American, low-income elementary school district in Northern California. Through a process of community nomination, eight teachers were selected on the basis of being identified by both parents and principals as outstanding teachers. The parents' criteria for teaching excellence included: being accorded respect by the teacher; student enthusiasm toward the school and academic tasks; and student attitudes toward themselves and others.

There were four phases to the study. The first consisted of an ethnographic interview to discuss teacher background, teaching philosophy, and notions about curriculum, classroom management, and parent and community involvement. In the second phase, teachers agreed to be observed by the researcher on an unscheduled basis at an average of three days a week, for a period of almost two years. The third phase involved videotaping the teachers in action. The last phase of the study required that the teachers work together as a research collaborative to view segments of one another's videotapes. In a series of ten 2–3 hour meetings, the teachers participated in analyses and interpretation of their own and their colleagues' practice. It was during this stage of the study that formulations about culturally relevant pedagogy that had emerged in the initial interviews were confirmed by practice.

The teachers in this study met a set of criteria. These criteria were: concrete experiences as a criterion of meaning; the use of dialogue in assessing knowledge

claims; the ethic of caring; the ethic of personal accountability; cultural critique; and cultural competence. These were thought to be appropriate criteria for helping their students to be academically successful, culturally competent, and sociopolitically critical. However, the different ways in which the teachers met these criteria led Ladson-Billings to search for commonalities that might exist in their theoretical perspectives which, when taken together, might define the concept and practice of culturally relevant teaching. Three broad commonalities were demonstrated:
- their conceptions of self and others
- the manner in which they structured social relations
- their conception of knowledge.

The chief beliefs and practices driving these commonalities are outlined in Table 6.1.

Table 6.1 Commonalities which define culturally relevant teaching

Conceptions of self and others	Structuring of social relations	Conceptions of knowledge
Believed that all students were capable of academic success. Saw their pedagogy as art— unpredictable always in the process of becoming. Saw themselves as members of the community. Saw teaching as a way to give back to the community.	Maintained fluid student–teacher relations. Demonstrated a connectedness with all of the students. Developed a community of learners. Encouraged students to learn collaboratively and be responsible for one another.	Believed that knowledge is not static, it is shared and constructed. Believed that knowledge must be viewed critically. Believed that teachers must be passionate about knowledge and learning— and must scaffold to facilitate learning. Believed that assessment must be multifaceted.

(Ladson-Billings, 1994)

The Grace Stanford study

An interpretative study carried out by Stanford (1997) of Pennsylvania University in Delaware builds on previous studies of exemplary African-American teachers, by portraying the beliefs and practices of four successful urban African-American teachers. In 1985, the Golden Apple Foundation was established in Chicago for the purpose of recognising and promoting excellence in teaching. Periodically, 10 teachers from within the Chicago metropolitan area are selected to receive awards. Teachers are nominated for an award by parents, community members, or colleagues. Nominees are required to submit essays on a set topic, along with three letters of recommendation. A selection committee composed of volunteer education professionals is responsible for reviewing the applications and selecting the 30 finalists. Each finalist is observed by a two-member team from the selection committee during a specified period of time, and each team also interviews administrators, parents, and colleagues. A written report is submitted and from there the committee selects 10 recipients for the award. In total, 13 African-American teachers received the award between 1985 and 1993. The four teachers selected for the Stanford study—three regular classroom teachers and one special education teacher—taught in schools with a student population comprised African-Americans from a low-income band, and their teaching spanned elementary through high school, as well as regular and special education. The Stanford study portrayed their beliefs and practices, within the context of effective African-American pedagogy. Four characteristics emerged:

- community solidarity (teacher closely identifies with students' community)
- community of learners (teacher established a learning community within the classroom)
- focus on the whole child (interest in students not limited to cognitive development)
- personal accountability (willingly took responsibility for students' learning and behaviour, despite the big challenges).

Both Casey (1993) and Ladson-Billings (1995) contend that African-American pedagogy determines that the teachers hold a strong sense of identity with the community in which they teach. This sense of identity results from a shared culture and, frequently, current or former residence within the school community, or a similar one, which enables the teachers to feel an attachment to the community. This trait prevailed among the teachers in the Stanford study.

One of the teachers relished the challenge of teaching students perceived as being "difficult" because, rather than focusing on the perceived limitations of the students, he looked at their unrealised potential for success. Much of this teacher's success came from the interpersonal relationships he established with the students. Those relationships were characterised by genuine respect and concern for their wellbeing. The students perceived his concern for them as a sign of respect, and responded by giving him their respect and co-operation. The positive social climate in the classroom enhanced the students' ability to achieve academically and to develop appropriate social skills. Similar traits and practices were evident in the other three teachers in the study.

Like Ladson-Billings (1995), Stanford discovered in her case studies that these teachers created a sense of community in their classrooms. For them, establishing a "community of learners" involved assuming familial roles in addition to the role of teacher. The classes were often described as being like a family. Their classes became a magnet for students, with one student commenting on the fact that students wanted to be there, because it was a safe haven with a presence of the human touch. One teacher stated, "I teach children, not subject matter."

All teachers in the study expected students to aspire to high academic and behaviour standards, but their interest in students was not limited to their cognitive development alone. They were interested in their students' social and emotional growth as well. This interest in the whole child was manifested in different ways by the teachers. These ranged from students sharing the teacher's life experiences to extending their education to beyond the classroom—for example, attending funerals, visiting jails, and supporting sports activities and community events.

Another common theme among the teachers in this study was their willingness to accept responsibility for teaching their students, even though they confronted challenging situations that frequently resulted in despair and resistance from other colleagues. Rather than wasting time complaining about inadequate resources, the teachers frequently used their own resources to provide necessary materials. Not one of the teachers sought to blame the students for any difficulties they were experiencing, either academically or socially. They did not speak disparagingly of their students' home environment or background. They accepted the students for who they were, and looked for ways to build on their strengths, thus creating a classroom environment which nurtured and sustained learning. They also derived a great deal of satisfaction from their successes with the students. One teacher, for example, stated that when they saw a student "blossoming out", it "just did something to me".

Stanford suggests that the success of these teachers replicates the findings of Ladson-Billings' (1995) studies on effective African-American pedagogy. Three significant characteristics which emerged from the Stanford study correspond to the common themes in similar research: a sense of community; a sense of holism; and a sense of accountability.

The Pauline Lipman study

Pauline Lipman of De Paul University builds on the idea that if schools are to value students from diverse backgrounds and support their academic success and cultural integrity, reformers must draw from the knowledge of successful teachers of such students. Her contention is reinforced largely by her research in two schools which were in the process of restructuring (Lipman, 1995).

From 1988 to 1991, Lipman applied ethnographic methods to study two restructuring Junior High Schools that had high numbers of African-American suspensions, and a punitive approach in many classrooms. One school's population was approximately 60 percent African-American; the other's was close to 80 percent. The percentage of African-American teachers in the schools was 16 percent (the lowest of any Junior High in the district) and 50 percent respectively. Yet both schools had a number of teachers who engaged otherwise alienated students in meaningful learning experiences. Lipman's study describes three of these teachers, based on her observations and interviews with them, who succeeded where their colleagues often failed.

While all three teachers in Lipman's study were African-American, it does not necessarily follow that culturally relevant teachers must be of the same culture as the student cohort (see Macfarlane, 2003; Pierce, 1996). Lipman unearthed commonalities amongst the three exemplary teachers, despite their different teaching styles and methods. They all:

- insisted on high academic and behaviour standards and worked to help children achieve them
- tapped into their students' experiences and culture, often in the process validating children's lives
- relentlessly coached students in the nuances of the dominant discourse without denigrating their home culture or challenging their identity
- took at-risk students under their wing and helped them negotiate tacit norms and expectations that other teachers take for granted
- perceived teaching as a calling, a responsibility not only to students and family but the community also
- provided the care and guidance that was often absent from students' daily lives
- transformed drab classrooms into their own lively and attractive spaces.

Lipman concluded that their connectedness with students and their mentoring evoked respect and academic effort from challenging and resistant students.

The Cecelia Pierce study

Cecelia Pierce (1996) reports on a case study that outlines how one effective teacher, teaching predominantly at-risk learners, created a classroom climate that enhanced learning outcomes for all students. Pierce, of the University of Alabama, centred her study on Mary Morgan (not her real name), a middle-school teacher with 24 years' teaching experience. Morgan's effectiveness in teaching at-risk students was defined by the recommendations of teachers, administrators, parents, and former students. Pierce observed Mary Morgan daily for 12 weeks in her classroom and recorded audiotapes and field notes. In particular, the researcher identified verbal and nonverbal teaching behaviours and patterns, teacher personality characteristics, and the ways in which these factors facilitated student learning. Using students as key informants, Pierce triangulated her observations and conclusions with those of the teacher and students to attest to the accuracy of recorded data.

The inner-city school in this study was located in the south-eastern United States, where the student population was predominantly Black. The class included 21 students, of whom 29 percent were White and 71 percent were Black.[1] Seventeen of the students had been identified as at-risk by the guidance counsellors and the teacher, based on their previous school performance and socioeconomic status. Pierce (1996) presumed that the majority of these students did not value education, a view reinforced by their parents. Consequently, they tended to exhibit hesitancy, fear, and insecurity when confronted with the demands of school, an observation also shared by researchers in other settings (Ashman & Elkins, 1998; Clark et al., 1996; Kauffman, 1997; McInerney & McInerney, 1998).

These attitudes, Mary Morgan maintained, needed to be countered and minimised by developing a classroom ambiance which increased opportunities for success, allowed opportunity for student participation in the learning process, and provided a safe haven for students. Pierce (1996) identified three key components in Mary Morgan's classroom which provided "safe-haven" status:

- a classroom organisation based upon correct standards of behaviour and sensitivity toward others
- a variety of roles assumed by the teacher to give support to the students
- the teacher's enthusiasm for the students.

---

1 The terms White and Black are used by the author in the academic journal article.

The chief beliefs and practices which underpinned these components are outlined in Table 6.2 below.

Table 6.2 Key components of the "safe-haven" status of Mary Morgan's classroom

Classroom organisation	Roles assumed by the teacher	Teacher's enthusiasm for students
Instilled in students a belief in their abilities to learn and a desire to achieve. Each child knew they were valued. Planned to bond into a co-operative unit at beginning of year. Ensured students understand and internalise the rules. Explain consequences of improper behaviour.	Teacher modelled the desired behaviour. Teacher as person, encourager, counsellor, and safety net. Teacher may share discerningly, his or her own experiences. Teacher is never threatening. Teacher skilled both in academic and non-academic dialogue.	Enthusiasm is developed from life experiences. Enthusiasm is developed from formal education experiences. Relaxed classroom atmosphere adds to enthusiastic climate. Freedom of (but controlled) movement within the classroom. Teacher's attention to students. Teacher's warm smile.

(Pierce, 1996)

Pierce (1996) concludes that Mary Morgan's classroom climate was premised primarily on specific behaviours, which nurtured the emotional needs of her students. Her intention to set the scene at the beginning of the year proved to be both proactive and preventive. The exhibiting of the desired behaviour by the teacher, and her focus on setting out rules and explanations at the beginning of the year, illustrate her commitment to classroom priorities of quality learning and behaviour. The benefits that accrued were academic as well as social. They confirmed a reduction of inappropriate classroom behaviour, an increase in attendance, and a reduction in the number of assignments not completed.

Te Kōtahitanga: the experiences of Years 9 and 10 Māori students in mainstream schools

In 2002, the Ministry of Education funded the Te Kōtahitanga project in order to ascertain how Māori students respond to and interpret the varying influences there are on their educational achievement and how they might see ways of improving their educational achievement (see Bishop, Berryman, Tiakiwai, & Richardson, 2002, 2003).

> The key focus of this overall project was not necessarily one of revisiting these influences as such, but rather seeking to investigate questions that flow from these accounts such as *how are these factors (and others not listed) experienced by the*

students? And how do these factors manifest themselves and play a part in what happens in the classroom? And how might an understanding of the dynamic nature of these influences indicate solutions to the problems facing Māori students in mainstream classrooms? (Ministry of Education, 2003, p. 3)

The project design has three key components. The first is to identify underlying teacher and school behaviours, assumptions, and attitudes that influence their attitudes towards Māori students. The second is to investigate how these are impacting on Māori students' achievement. The third is to understand Māori students' experiences in the classroom with a view to informing policy, teaching and learning, in order to enhance engagement and achievement (outcomes) for Māori students.

During this research project, kaupapa Māori research principles (Bishop, 1996a) were followed to address issues of power, initiative, benefits, representation, legitimation, and accountability, in the research relationship. This framework provided the conceptual basis both for the development of the research methods and for the evaluation of the data gathered. A scoping exercise was conducted within a range of schooling types in mid 2001, and a set of testable hypotheses was conducted. These hypotheses guided the research team to develop and trial specific learning and teaching strategies across several specific sites and in several different curriculum areas.

The research approach, termed "collaborative storying" (Bishop, 1996b), involved a sequence of in-depth, semistructured interviews as conversations, and facilitated the differing voices and theorisings of the research participants being heard. The findings revealed that:

- The teachers spoke of students' deficiencies as being major barriers to students' progress and achievement.
- Parents and students, by contrast, identified a combination of structural and cultural relationship barriers that limited students' satisfactory progress and achievement.
- Factors limiting the achievement of Māori students within classrooms included teacher–student relationships, pedagogical interactions between teacher and student, the dynamics of the teaching and learning process, and the effects of peers.

The Te Kōtahitanga project produced a series of narratives of experience covering a range of schools, decile levels, and demographic details. The narratives were developed by way of interviews at four school sites, four principals, 80 teachers, 70 students, and 50 parents. From the student narratives, and with support from the narratives of the parents, the principals, and some of the teachers, an Effective Teaching Profile was developed.

Effective teachers of Māori students demonstrate that they care for students. On a daily basis, they demonstrate this care by manifesting such qualities as respect, compassion, understanding of a student's worldview, fairness, friendliness, and a sense of humour (see also Hill & Hawk, 2000; Ladson-Billings, 1995; Lipman, 1995; Macfarlane, 1995, 1997, 2002, 2004; Pierce, 1996; Stanford, 1997). Bishop et al. (2003) go on to explain how teaching interactions might be effective, and provide examples of how many of the characteristics listed above might be carried out in the culturally relevant learning environment.

The Te Kōtahitanga project has provided professional development in many schools with a focus on reducing or eliminating deficit theorising about Māori students, improving teacher–student relationships, building on in-school and community expertise, and identifying the structural changes that need to be addressed. According to Bishop and Berryman (2006), it sends out a clear and unequivocal message to all involved in education in New Zealand: "culture speaks".

Making a difference in the classroom: effective teaching practice in low-decile, multicultural schools

The Achievement in Multicultural High Schools (AIMHI) project was established by the Ministry of Education in New Zealand as part of its schooling improvement policy. The project was based on the strategic plan for Pacific Islands Education "Ko e Ako 'a e Kakai Pasifika" and was officially launched in 1995.

The Ministry invited eight secondary schools to participate in the project. The participation criteria included being in the decile 1 category, and having a high proportion of Pasifika students. Data collected on the ethnicity of the students in the schools made it immediately clear that all the schools had significant numbers of students who were Māori. Seven of the schools are located in Auckland and one in Wellington.

The aims of the project were to:
- increase the market share of students attending the participating schools
- raise the levels of performance of the schools and students in the following areas:

- high student achievement
- strong governance and management
- strong school/community relationships
- integrated social service support
* achieve sustainable self-managing schools. (Hill & Hawk, 2000, p. 1)

Over a six-month period, the researchers observed 100 lessons involving 89 teachers in a broad range of subjects across year levels. Close to twelve "effective" teachers were selected from each school, on the basis of their credibility as perceived by their colleagues and students, for the quality of their classroom management skills as well as for their classroom instruction, social interactions, and teaching and learning interactions. To facilitate triangulation of the data gathered in the observations, each was followed by an interview with the teacher and a group discussion with approximately six students from each of the classes observed. The work carried out by the researchers in the classrooms was guided by data from the original baseline document that outlined the particular qualities and skills of teachers as perceived by teachers and students. The observations provided an opportunity to make links between what was perceived to be happening in classrooms (espoused practice) and what was actually observed (actual practice). Hill and Hawk (2000) provide the following description in their report to the Ministry of Education:

> There was a high degree of consistency in the way the teachers in the sample thought and felt about their work as teachers. As well as being professional and highly skilled they are very positive and optimistic. They perform with a confidence that gives their students a confidence in them and they want to solve problems rather than putting up barriers to progress. These teachers are hard working and bring a certain energy to their teaching that creates a sense of urgency and purpose in their classrooms. They are not afraid to share power with students and work hard to divest the locus of control to students rather than keep it themselves.
>
> The data shows that these students have particular needs that students in other schools do not have. The relationship that students in these schools form with their teacher is crucial. While the relationship that forms between a student and a teacher in any school is important, the data in this study shows that it is not only important to these students but is a prerequisite for learning. If a teacher has not been able to form a positive relationship of reciprocal respect the students in that class will find it very, very difficult to be motivated to learn. The teachers in this study had particular understandings and attitudes that make it easier for these

relationships to be positive and strong. One of the most important dimensions to the relationship is the respect the teachers have for the students. The students described how the body language, tone of voice and the actions of these teachers showed the students that these teachers did not want a 'power over' relationship but 'power with' their students. The students felt that these teachers treated them as people and adults rather than students or children and, because their relationships are based on notions of reciprocity, the students respected these teachers in return. These teachers understood the various worlds the students live in and how they manage the tensions and conflicts between them, they were fair and patient, enjoyed participating in activities with the students, and were prepared to give themselves—share their lives, feelings, failings and vulnerabilities with the students. (p. ii)

As in corresponding New Zealand studies (in particular Bishop et al., 2003; Macfarlane, 2003; Macfarlane, Glynn, Cavanagh, & Bateman, 2005), relationships—between teachers and students, and amongst students—were found to be critical. Students felt safe in environments that had these characteristics, and they were keener to contribute, to take risks, and to manifest interest and enjoyment in their learning activities. Student motivation and attitudes were enhanced on account of a number of factors, including team building and cohesion early in the school year, a high level of planning, and enthusiastic teacher support. Teachers modelled the desired behaviours and regularly made time to teach relationship skills. These teachers also orchestrated their classroom activities in such a way as to ensure smooth transitions, good tempo, and busyness. Students in AIMHI schools also responded well to routines, and openly respected teachers who took a no-nonsense approach to classroom issues and expectations. Humour was also a trait that these teachers had.

Student feedback indicated that each of the schools had a number of teachers whose performance is not meeting students' expectations. It is imperative that teacher needs are accurately identified through a comprehensive process, employing methods such as observations and student feedback. This needs to be followed up with targeted development and careful monitoring. Based on the research findings, it is argued strongly that a number of performance standards need to be developed that guide and determine what is required of teachers. Some key themes from this study are that effective teachers understand their students—their world, who they are—and that they are fair, and giving of themselves (Hill & Hawk, 2000).

What makes an exceptional teacher: culturally responsive teaching

According to Rutter et al. (1979), a range of specific skills is demonstrated by effective teachers. They report on teachers who work at perfecting their craft. Active engagement in learning is a fundamental element of good teaching and learning identified by Māori students in the Te Kōtahitanga project (Bishop et al., 2003; Bishop & Berryman, 2006). In other words, teachers need to be fine technicians.

Exceptional teachers, however, are excellent communicators as well as fine technicians. To be such, the instruction has to be predicated on culturally responsive pedagogy. This has been described earlier as a style of teaching that takes into account students' cultural background, and acknowledging how they learn—not to be confused with deriving *content* from culture. Teaching African-American students about Martin Luther King Jnr, or teaching Māori students about the great Te Kooti, is not necessarily culturally responsive, however useful and worthwhile these topics are. Culturally responsive teaching is about allowing students to bring their cultural experiences and realities to the context upon which knowledge and skills are developed.

From the studies previously outlined in this chapter, it can be confidently maintained that the exceptional teachers they report on drew on the culture of their students to enhance their engagement in the learning activities. It could also be maintained that the teachers were responsive to culture while maintaining the essential elements of successful classroom environments. These essential elements include: having a structured curriculum; sustaining a challenging, academic focus; having reasonable expectations of students' performance; insisting on quality in terms of producing the best that they can do; and emphasising crisp transitions from one activity to the next.

An AIMHI hero

Some classroom observations and interviews were carried out on an individual teacher who was a participant in Hill and Hawk's (2000) AIMHI project (Macfarlane, 2004). This teacher was non-Māori (note the analogy to Mary Morgan of the Pierce (1996) study), aged 35, and in his fifth year of teaching at the time of the observations. The school he taught at was in South Auckland. This school is a multicultural, coeducational state school of some 900 students, with a large Pasifika and Māori student representation.

For one day a week over a school term in 2001, visits were made to his classroom to observe the pedagogical practices that were carried out there. This teacher impressed in terms of the structures that he put in place and the way he orchestrated the classroom activities. His meticulous planning and lesson momentum were underscored by manaakitanga. Manaakitanga was manifested by creating an ethic of care in the classroom. He showed the students that he cared by good teaching and maintaining a positive attitude. The students knew that they were valued, and because Māori and Pasifika students acknowledge reciprocity, they valued their teacher in return. The class had posters on the walls that reflected the students' community, their sporting icons, and the heroes and heroines that were known to them. Their teacher was also visible in the community, taking an active role in the homework centre at the local youth library, attending sporting fixtures, shopping at the local supermarket, and attending the local church.

Observing this teacher at work in his classroom, it soon became obvious that his style bore a rather uncanny resemblance to the "four rules of classroom management" proposed by Smith and Laslett (1993): get them in; get on with it; get on with them; move them on.

As each form class arrived, this teacher quite often waited near the doorway to greet and direct the students, if necessary, to a seating location. He advance organised, and started promptly. Always well planned, he knew the content well; his communication skills sent out messages that he was alert, keeping the students attentive. He also maintained sound procedures for closing and dismissing. However, the way in which Smith and Laslett's four rules were operationalised was not identically applied to each of the classes he taught. The level of the class, and also the class personnel, were influential factors.

What else did this teacher do to show that he was genuine about sustaining effective peadagogigical practices with his secondary school classes? In what ways were messages of care extended to his students? It is clear that he:
- set goals that were realistic, and explained the rationale for the topic
- set goals that could be accomplished, often within a reasonable time period. (For some classes, a unit of study lasting six weeks was too long and drawn out. This presented the risk of the study losing its impetus, the students losing interest, and the teacher losing credibility.)
- reinforced little and often

- worked at the student's level, for example kneeling at the table and working with an individual student or a small group, while simultaneously scanning the room from time to time
- directed attention equitably, avoiding becoming too involved with one student for too long
- planned meticulously, helping to create a no-nonsense, task-oriented ethos
- worked from a range of vantage points in the room, avoiding standing too often at the front or sitting behind his desk
- marked the students' work. Teachers who don't attend to this are sending out messages that they don't care. Where is the manaakitanga in that? What will that do to and for the teaching and learning dynamics?
- used a vernacular that suited the context. Most students, it seems, thrive better in an environment where moderate language, balanced emotions, and clear explanations are the norm.

Finally, this teacher had a principal (leader) who took an active role in encouraging him, and the rest of his staff, to develop their careers as educators of a diverse cohort of students. To this end, regular whole-staff professional development courses were provided. Staff were encouraged to report on their work by presenting at academic conferences and maintaining interactions with staff from colleges of education and universities. Good leaders understand the various strengths and skills that each of their staff bring with them, and they acknowledge those skills and encourage their teachers to expand on them. This principal opened doors for enthusiastic and innovative members of staff, never losing sight of the real purposes of schooling, foremost among those being students' achievement.

Summary

A number of studies, from the USA and New Zealand, have reported on good teachers and good teaching, and have offered profiles of what good teachers and good teaching look like. The similarities of their findings with regard to good teaching are too marked to be mere coincidence. What these teachers did in their classrooms, and how they infused elements of sensitivity and sensibility into their practice, were what made a difference for their students in terms of their attitudes and performance. Student engagement in learning is linked to such factors as relevant content, challenging work, receiving good feedback, and learning that takes place at the students' pace. Student engagement in school also indicated strong links to home support, supportive friendships, and having interests that extended individuals.

The exemplars of good practice cited in this chapter endorse the notion that effective teachers have specific knowledge and skills which successfully work with students. In other words, they have the right balance of such skills and knowledge combined with their own personality traits. In the face of the current outcry about student failure and school strife, exemplars of this kind may offer some relief. Teachers such as those introduced in this chapter serve to make real the axiom that educators need to approach the practice of teaching as a moral craft—an approach that effectively brings into play the heart, the head, and the hand (Sergiovanni, 1994). The heart is about having a philosophy and therefore incorporates beliefs, values, and vision. The head involves personal or cognitive theory. The hand is about practices—the skills, strategies, and decisions that are both concrete and emphatic. Each without the other two denotes vulnerability. Each with the other two denotes authority.

CHAPTER 7

The Hikairo Rationale:
a culturally responsive approach for working with students with behaviour difficulties

Introduction

A central theme underlying the principle of equity in education is the role that culture plays in the lives of people, and the implications of that role for those involved in working with students and their whānau. Sensitivities to the cultural background and experiences of identifiable groups of people is especially important in today's diverse society. Since culture is a product of learning, the cultural dispositions that both teacher and learner bring to the pedagogical process are also important. Teachers who are sensitive to cultural dynamics will be able to understand and respond better to the development of students with learning and behaviour difficulties. Axelson (1993) contends that basic social expressions such as language, norms, sanctions, and values convey a great deal about the cultural context of any group of people. It seems reasonable, therefore, to expect educators to have grasped an awareness of and respect for these social expressions, in order for good teacher–student relationships to be advanced with earnest. A lack of awareness or respect for the particular social expressions that students bring with them into the classroom is unacceptable and regrettable. At best, such a stance would neutralise the relationship-building process; at worst, it has the potential to destroy the relationship.

In terms of teaching in diverse settings, and particularly where students with behaviour difficulties are present, a culture-based approach requires that the appropriateness of existing educational theories be adapted or reworked (if necessary) to meet the personal needs of individuals. The positioning of mainstream culture comes from the dominant group of people. Axelson (1993) asserts that an individual who belongs primarily to the dominant group may encounter any collection of issues or challenges, but the minority group individual will be affected not only by the same set of issues and challenges, but also by those that are particular to their own distinctive (minority) group.

In some way or at some level, most people face issues related to community and political activities, education and academic progress, and social and personal development. Inevitably, one's cultural identity is the frame of reference through which these issues are viewed. This frame of reference is the cultural toolkit that one carries and through which one derives patterns of meaning that enhance an individual's effectiveness. It seems timely that a bicultural approach to supporting students with learning and behaviour difficulties be developed, so that the quality of the learning environment might be enhanced and enriched.

Designing the Hikairo Rationale

The front page of the *Education Weekly* of 30 January 1995 referred to the rising level of violence in New Zealand schools. Comparisons were made with the situation in the United States, where 26 percent of students admitted to having carried a weapon to school within a given 30-day period (*Education Weekly*, 1995). The New Zealand picture is not quite so bleak. The Ministry of Education, and schools themselves, have introduced initiatives that are intended to address many of the issues that arise when students' behaviour problems escalate. Nonetheless, there were 20,447 stand-down cases during 2004, at a rate of 27 per 1,000 students. This is the same as the 2003 rate. The most common reasons for suspension were continual disobedience (26 percent) and drugs (26 percent). There were 4,774 suspension cases in 2004, a rate of 6.56 per 1,000 students. This is slightly lower than the 2003 rate of 6.75 per 1,000 students. The most common reasons for stand-down were continual disobedience (25 percent), physical assault on other students (25 percent), and verbal assault on staff (16 percent). The peak age for stand-downs and suspensions is 14 years (Ministry of Education, 2005).

Male students continue to represent the majority of stand-down and suspension cases, and most of these are in the 13–15 age group. A detailed breakdown of the figures for school suspensions shows that Māori students are, with monotonous regularity, grossly and disproportionately overrepresented. If account is taken of the fact that Māori students tend to drop out of school at a much earlier age than non-Māori students, the figures become even more disturbing.

One conclusion that might be drawn from these figures is that (some) schools are microcosms of wider society, and reflect widely held attitudes, preferring to punish and remove those students they deem to be unacceptable, or incompatible with the "norm" for the student population. While the Ministry of Education points out that rates for stand-downs and suspensions of Māori students are continuing to reduce, Drewery (2004) expresses highly relevant concerns:

> We could ask, what is wrong with Māori, and boys, and low socio-economic groups that they seem to get into so much more trouble. Equally we could ask, what is it about our schools that brings this situation about? Is it possible that there is something in the way schools go about their business that makes it easier for middle and upper socio-economic groups to conform than other groups? (p. 333)

The first concern is whether schools are providing appropriate support for Māori students. Undoubtedly, many schools are doing so. However, for a large number of schools, it appears that the principles of equity prescribed in their charters may be no more than empty promises. This highlights a second concern: how to provide additional and targeted support for teachers in New Zealand schools, as they try to make sense of situations that are often both highly charged and personally stressful.

The Hikairo Rationale addresses many of those concerns. It is not intended to be viewed as a handbook that provides "fix it" strategies for students experiencing learning and behaviour difficulties. No such document exists, nor is it ever likely to exist. Nor is it a replacement for the fine behaviour-management models outlined previously. What is offered here is a rationale which both recognises Māoritanga, and embraces those philosophies and practices which are indeed useful when dealing with young people who need support with their education.

From the outset it should be noted that this rationale, while having an educational focus, is also a tribute to a tipuna (tribal ancestor). In accordance with traditional protocol, permission was sought and granted to refer to this ancestor by the Ngāti Rangiwewehi Runanga (H. Hahunga, personal communication, 24 September 1997), prior to the original publication a decade ago. The Hikairo Rationale is so named because of the way peaceful resolution was reached following an intertribal encounter on Mokoia Island in 1823. According to Stafford (1967), the Ngāti Rangiwewehi Chief, Hikairo, spoke and acted with such mana and influence that the illustrious leaders of the day declared that aggression should make way for order. On this occasion, Hikairo's assertive dialogue, fundamental assurances, and simple sincerity brought about a change of attitude and behaviour. That single juncture in history is the source of the thinking that underpins this approach to working with students who are experiencing learning and behaviour difficulties in schools.

The Hikairo Rationale is appropriate for working with both Māori and non-Māori students and teachers, even though its guiding values and metaphors come from within a Māori world view. One fundamental Māori value, aroha (love), has a very real place in the model. Aroha does not mean a soft approach. In the context of discipline, aroha connotes co-operation, understanding, reciprocity, and warmth. The Hikairo Rationale espouses these qualities in abundance, while emphasising that a level of assertiveness needs to be infused simultaneously. This approach worked in 1883, and it can work today.

There are seven elements that comprise the rationale, each personified by the letters that form the spelling of H-I-K-A-I-R-O (see Figure 7.1). While each of the elements of the rationale may give the impression that they stand alone, that is not the case. The elements overlap and interweave in such a way that an interdependent strength and sustenance prevails. From time to time, however, one element will predominate, because within that dimension a particular set of skills and attitudes that best modify or explain a particular teaching and learning situation will be the focus.

Further, because the instructional environment is a dynamic one, influenced by biological, academic, social, and cultural factors, the elements of the Hikairo Rationale are not to be interpreted in a linear order, as portrayed in Figure 7.1. The elements each provide a means for describing and responding to a range of learning and behaviour phenomena that teachers encounter in today's diverse classrooms. In the Hikairo Rationale, each element is represented by way of a fundamental Māori principle, perhaps best illustrated in the form of Te Rākau (Figure 7.2).

Figure 7.1 The Hikairo Rationale

Huakina mai	Opening doorways
Ihi	Being assertiveness
Kōtahitanga	Seeking collaboration
Awhinatia	Helping learners
I runga i te manaaki	Caring that pervades
Rangatiratanga	Motivating learners
Orangatanga	Nurturing environment

Figure 7.2 Te Rākau

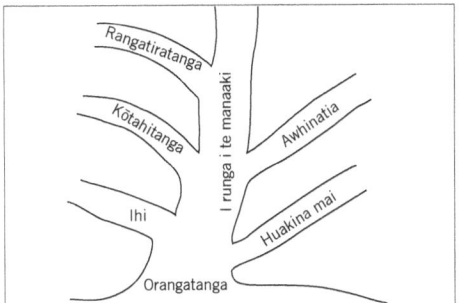

Te Rākau

In Māoridom, as in other cultures, the tree is a symbol of strength and life. Māori mythology sees people as families originating from Tane Mahuta, the father of forests, plants, and humankind. The seven elements of Te Rākau have orangatanga (developing a nurturing environment) as the base, depicted here as the roots of the tree. The arteries of the tree trunk represent another element, that of manaaki (growing a caring community). This is significant, because the ethos of care must be pervasive if any environment is to thrive. Branching out from the caring centre are the five other elements: huakina mai (opening doorways); ihi (being assertive); kōtahitanga (linking home and school); awhinatia (moving toward restorative practice); and rangatiratanga (motivating learners). Like a tree, all people have basic needs that they strive to fulfil, and students are more likely to behave appropriately when these needs are met.

Huakina mai: the Hikairo approach for opening doorways

Although the specific causes of misunderstandings occurring in schools differ, depending upon the context, there is one common element: polarised communication. Gudykunst (1994) contends that polarised communication exists when groups or individuals promote self-interest, and have little or no regard for the interests of others. Many teachers inadvertently or unknowingly express levels of intolerance in their conversations with their colleagues and students. Disinterest in or even a sense of disconnectedness with the backgrounds of others only serves to stultify communication and harm the communication process.

As a starting point for opening doorways in a culturally responsive way, teachers, both Māori and non-Māori, need to know about the iwi (tribe) and hapū (subtribe) that are tangata whenua (local people) in the school's district. They also need to know about tribal stories and protocol, talk to local people, digest this information, and, when ready, experience the parts of it that they are comfortable with.

Take the hypothetical case of a person who moved from their tribal area of Te Arawa to the Waikato tribal area. Although this person did have some degree of knowledge of the Tainui waka (ancestral canoe) and its iwi, it was not considerable. In view of the fact that this person would be working in a context with a strong Waikato profile, becoming familiar with some of the history, icons, and people became a priority. Reading and talking to others about the kīngitanga, poukai (pilgrimage), Princess Te Puea (an iconic ancestor), raupatu (dispossession), the river of bends and esoteric minders (Waikato taniwharau, he piko he taniwha), and observing and participating in hui (gatherings) at local marae, proved both helpful and useful. These activities made this person more aware of and insightful about the tribe's trials, tribulations, sources of pride, and successes. Becoming aware required diligence and commitment, but it did not require that this person become one of them; that cannot be. However, knowing more about the tangata whenua status brought about a sense of being at ease and comfortable within and among them. It is no different for teachers, who need to build relationships by taking the time to learn about students' backgrounds, as well as the backgrounds of the local Māori iwi (Macfarlane, 2004).

Educators are able to respond to challenging student behaviour by creating opportunities to establish meaningful relationships even prior to the first day in the classroom or school. Being proactive will reduce the need to be reactive. The narratives already attached to many students within the education system may create a preconceived and negative bias in teachers. Students with behaviour difficulties are regularly labelled bad, unco-operative, uncouth, deviant, arrogant, aggressive, or a combination of these. The labels develop into "stories" which, in the main, precede the student's arrival in a new year level or learning environment. To add more words to the story is unfair and unacceptable, as it represents the perpetuation of student disadvantage, where the individual is forced to operate under limiting and encumbering conditions socially, psychologically, and educationally.

Proactive teachers choose to destroy the myths that accompany particular students by focusing on the behaviour, not the person. A proactive teacher who discovers that a student "storied" in this way will become a member of the class makes arrangements to meet with the student, prior to the first day in the new setting. The tenor of the teacher's approach is one of control, affection, and faith, for example: "I know you will be starting class with us next week and I just want to let you know that we're looking forward to you becoming part of the whānau [classroom community]. We'll work together a lot, as we want to make this a special year . . ."

From the outset, it is crucial that the teacher gets to know the student and that the student is aware of the teacher's expectations. For those students who, unfortunately, have a reputation for being difficult, the opening of doorways must occur at the earliest point.

Parents and students need to be involved in discussions affecting them. Activities and decisions that are planned must include their full consultation and participation in the decision making (Gadd, 1976). Parental participation is an indispensable ingredient for academic and social progress. Winzer and Mazurek (1998) assert that the closer a parent is to the education of his or her child, the greater the potential impact will be on the educational achievement of the child. The gains can be numerous. Some of these gains may relate to academic progress, fewer discipline issues, enhanced self-esteem and social skills, better attendance, and improved attitude.

There are no hard and fast rules for involving Māori parents in their children's schooling. Reactions and interactions between Māori parents and the school differ greatly. The following suggestions are helpful when interacting with and engaging Māori parents:

- Find out about the families' backgrounds, their marae, their iwi.
- Visit the home, remembering that a positive phone call needs to precede the visit. Don't deliver negative feedback over the phone.
- Check whether parents are comfortable with your ideas, actions, or intentions.
- Be up front if you lack confidence in terms of cultural awareness. Tell parents about your knowledge gaps and that you may make unintentional mistakes.
- Be personable, warm, and respectful. Many Māori parents have a strong aversion to being confronted with disparaging and demeaning commentary.
- Use everyday, jargon-free language in the conversations.
- Initial contact with parents should be just that, initial contact. A protracted

first visit is a no-no. So be firm, be brief, be gone. (This is also a good classroom discipline strategy.)

Scenario example: Quinton

Quinton Taylor (not his real name), a well built Māori boy aged 13, with the reputation of being a tough student who has left a trail of despair behind him, has been stood-down for verbally abusing a teacher. He is due to return to school after a three-day probation. A collaborative decision has been made to move him into a different home room class, 3 DT. The class teacher is Mr Thomson, who is non-Māori, but has developed and maintained an interest in te reo and tikanga Māori (language and customs). Quinton's whānau affiliates to the local iwi. Mr Thomson starts by finding out about Quinton's whānau, the marae to which the whānau belongs, Quinton's sporting interests, and his strengths. He then comes up with a simple plan for opening doorways (huakina mai) for this student and his whānau. He will do this by being purposeful, clear, resolute, fair, and by getting in early.

The first part of the plan involves a home visit to introduce himself. The second part involves a more formal meeting where class expectations are explained and clarified. The third part centres on involving a tuakana (senior student) as a temporary mentor to support Quinton.

Mr Thomson phones Quinton's mother to organise an appointment. Initially, she is quite evasive, their conversation progressing along the following lines:

Mr Thomson Kia ora Mrs Taylor, I am Dan Thomson from Quinton's school.

Remember, the teacher is not Māori, but he commences with the simple, yet commonly uttered phrase in Māoridom. Many non-Māori teachers may not realise that such a gesture has a significant and positive impact:

Mother Kia ora Mr Thomson. Oh, this is about my son?

Mr Thomson suspects a little quiver in her voice; there appears to be a level of fear or anticipation on her part.

Mr Thomson Quinton is coming into my Year 9 home room and I need to come and talk to him before he returns to school on Monday.

Mother When would you like to do that, and where?

Mr Thomson Today, after school if possible. At home or at school, your choice.

Mr Thomson needs to make three attempts to set up an appointment time with Mrs Taylor before a date and time are confirmed. Mrs Taylor may have good reasons for being somewhat elusive. For a long time, her interactions with school personnel have been built on deficit theorising around her son. However, Mr Thomson is persistent. He is adamant that this meeting take place, and his persistence pays off.

The following day he arrives at the agreed time of 4 pm He introduces himself and shares some of his own background, including how long he has been teaching and his main teaching interests. He asks if her husband, Wally, is still working at the local sawmill and if the whānau has regular contact with Piki Mai marae. Mr Thomson has done his homework; he has made connections with whānau affiliations and activities, shared some of himself and his experiences, and he started to earn their trust. Small talk is important talk in conversations with Māori—it sets the scene. Too often, professionals wish to go directly to the topic in hand, whereas many Māori prefer the indirect or ecological pathway.

In a matter of minutes Quinton appears on the scene, and Mr Thomson directs his attention to him. He makes eye contact, shakes hands, congratulates Quinton on a good rugby league result the previous Sunday (he has found out about his sporting prowess), asks who his team is playing the following weekend, and wishes him well for the game. Quinton begins to trust this person who is going to be his new teacher. But there are two more phases of the plan to implement.

The more formal but not overly prescribed meeting takes place after school the following day. Quinton, Mrs Taylor, and Mr Thomson meet in the home room. This is the teacher's opportunity to share with Quinton and his whānau some of the rules and expectations that are part of his classroom's protocol. After covering the peripheral information, Mr Thomson moves on to outline the class rules. Each person present is handed a sheet of paper giving these rules:

> Mr Thomson Here's the first one, Quinton: 'Attendance at class is important. Students must be on time and ready to start work.' Your attendance has been good all year, so do I hear you telling me that you will be on time and present?

This is an important rule, as students with severe and challenging behaviour tend to appear in the statistics as the late arrivers and the truants. Quinton did have a sound attendance record (to the despair of some of his previous teachers?), so Mr Thomson was expecting an affirmative response:

Quinton Yes, sir.

Mr Thomson No gang regalia here, Quinton. You look sharp now and you need to keep that standard of dress up. Okay Quinton?

Quinton Okay sir.

The influence of gangs on students of Quinton's age is a major concern to both educators and parents. Students with a reputation for being tough are often viewed as prospects by gang members. There is no evidence that Quinton had any such links, so Mr Thomson does not dwell on this issue. However, he needs to clarify his expectations and cover this important base:

Mr Thomson All students here have to participate in any organised activities. These include sport, camps, noho marae.

Quinton Sir, I like those activities.

Mr Thomson I know you do, and that pleases me, and your whānau too. However, this term, let's raise the bar.

Although this does not appear to be an obstacle in Quinton's case, Mr Thomson knows that students with severe and challenging behaviour often avoid organised activities when they are often the very ones who need those activities the most. It is a positive decision to include that point. Notice also that even before Quinton becomes a class member, the teacher is expecting him to extend himself.

Mr Thomson then moves on to the final and most critical point:

Mr Thomson I would like you to read the last rule, Quinton. (*If Quinton reads out the rule, there is a better chance that he will internalise the message.*)

Quinton (*Reading*) I must be courteous to staff at all times.

Mr Thomson What do you take the word courteous to mean, Quinton?

Quinton Respect, I think.

Mr Thomson In this class, students must be courteous. They must be respectful toward other students, property, and teachers. If this is going to be your class, then it is expected that you will do that, and especially show respect toward staff. Kōrero mai (talk to me), Quinton.

Quinton I don't know if I can do that, sir. (*Quinton is unsure if he will be able to unequivocally comply with the rule regarding respect.*)

Mr Thomson Thank you Quinton, for being honest with me. (*Gives a reinforcer*)

Mr Thomson uses a reinforcer rather than a censure. As Mr Thomson is well aware, Quinton has a history of verbally abusing teachers. He feels it is extremely courageous of Quinton to answer with such honesty in this instance, rather than simply setting out to appease those in the meeting by providing a response that he believes the adults would wish to hear, but which he does not mean. Quinton also knows that he has had trouble with compliance and has regularly got offside with several of his teachers. When students build up trust in a teacher they tend to be honest with him or her. It is apparent that seeds of trust are budding here, between Quinton and Mr Thomson.

The teacher then probes and talks about the support that will be provided to help Quinton build resilience and self-management skills, particularly in teacher–student interactions. Others in the room pledge support. Eventually, Quinton assures Mr Thomson that he will give it his best shot. The meeting has run its course.

Mr Thomson has arranged for tea and sandwiches in his room following the meeting. He has also arranged for Quinton's tuakana, Maru, to join them for refreshments. Quinton is initially rather aloof with Maru, until he discovers his mentor is also a keen rugby league player.

Another strategy for getting in early and manifesting fairness is to implement an unwritten fairness contract between teacher and students. This comes in the form of a clear statement from the teacher. The meaning of the statement is explained clearly to the students, modelled by the teacher, and reiterated where necessary (for example, if an individual or the group transgresses) at subsequent intervals. The expression is straightforward, for example: "I promise you that as long as you are part of this whānau (classroom), I will always be fair to you. Always. All I want in return is that you are fair to me. Do we have an understanding?"

This is not to say that a statement such as this will determine that fairness will always prevail—that would be far too simplistic. However, what it does say to students is that their teacher is not afraid of giving assurances to those in his or her care. It also signals that reciprocity is of significant value. When a teacher claims such an intention, it is imperative that this is honoured. Students know who the fair teachers are, and will be more likely to invest their respect in them. Fair teachers, quite simply, open doorways.

A respected Ngāti Rangiwewehi leader, a descendant of Hikairo, opens doorways for people in many ways. For over 20 years, his most significant contribution to education and society has been the provision of a wānanga (place of higher learning) that he co-ordinates on Mokoia Island, an iconic landmark in the rohe (district) of Te Arawa. The wānanga is open to people of all ages and ethnicities, but over the years it has been the anchorage for students who are experiencing turbulence in their lives. The core curriculum on this wānanga is based on traditional Māori arts and humanities. The curriculum is designed to respond to the learning and behaviour needs of students by allowing them to encounter, experience, and embrace the unique cultural meanings and symbols available to them by simply being who they are, Māori. Those who attend the wānanga and are non-Māori also have their own culture affirmed, as well as creating opportunities for accessing many of the finer elements of Māoritanga. The leader of this wānanga employs another, more direct version of huakina mai that deserves some commentary.

At the outset, prior to the boat leaving for the island, a karakia is recited, followed by brief whaikōrero (speech) by kaumātua. The teacher then says to the group of students, "Ko au ko koe, ko koe, ko au. Ko tāua. I am you and you are me. You and I together." A door of cultural connectedness is opened. There is a Māori connection; there is also a human connection.

A non-Māori teacher may well question the value—even the implications—of this approach, given that it is not immediately obvious that cultural connectedness would be possible. Indeed, there is another way to frame that statement, so that the concept of huakina mai can be meaningful within a bicultural context: "Ko au ko au—I am who I am. Ko koe ko koe—you are who you are. Ko tāua—let us move forward together."

There are numerous ways of opening doors for students. Most of the 730,000 students attending New Zealand's 2,700 schools will be able to identify a teacher who has opened the way forward for them. However, for many students, particularly those with learning and behaviour difficulties, the door is often jammed. The element of huakina mai is essential, because it lets these students know that they are valued by their teacher. It is a welcoming approach, consciously and strategically planned.

Ka tō he rā, ka rere he rā
A sun sets, a day is born

Ihi: being assertive

Assertive communication, properly employed, is a powerful strategy for responding to behaviour difficulties. Ihi (assertiveness) refers to the ability people have to act in their own and others' best interests, to stand up for their beliefs without undue anxiety, to express honest feelings comfortably, or to exercise personal rights without denying the rights of others (Alberti & Emmons, 1986). For many years, Lee and Marlene Canter have been refining their Assertive Discipline system. Charles (2002) contends that these authors popularised the concepts that teachers and students have the right to a calm and safe environment. Earlier the Canters focused on teachers being strong leaders in the classroom. More recently the emphasis on strong leadership has been complemented by the focus on building trusting and supportive relationships between teachers and students.

As a communication style and strategy, assertiveness is easily distinguishable from authoritarianism, and is in strong contrast to passivity. It reflects self-esteem and is considered to be a notable and important communication skill. Passive communicators do not define their personal boundaries, and place themselves at risk from more authoritarian people, who may unduly influence them. They are also typically less likely to attempt to influence others. The balance of power proposed by theories of student discipline (Porter, 2000) places autocratic-authoritarian approaches at one end of the continuum, and permissive *laissez-faire* approaches at the other. Porter explains that authoritarian teachers place rigid and often unrealistic boundaries or limits on students' behaviour, and impose strong sanctions for violating these. External controls are used by authoritarian teachers. The other extreme is an overly permissive approach. There is a strong argument in favour of an approach situated on what Porter (2000) refers to as "The Middle Ground" (p. 12). In this setting, power is more equally shared, rather than controls being imposed on students by the teacher, and self-discipline is encouraged.

Because assertiveness is such an encompassing concept, it is closely intertwined with and guided by a teacher's personality, individual students' nuances, and the overall mood of the class at any given time. The mood of the class may often determine a teacher's inclination to be in charge in some instances, or to adopt a softer position in other instances. These variances should not happen too frequently, as students prefer a teacher who demonstrates a consistent approach towards their classroom-management style.

In the Māori world, kaumātua (elders) and kaikōrero (orators) provide powerful models of assertiveness. On the marae, they excel in terms of self-expression, honesty, directness, and openness. They also excel in delivering messages tailored to a specific audience and a particular context. Assertive communication is an essential part of Māori protocol. According to Marsden (1975), ihi is a personal quality present in all human beings, but more developed in some than in others. Tate (1990) links the concept of ihi to the concept of mana. The assertive quality of ihi can be a manifestation of a person's mana, so that mana is not simply charisma, but also a force that can bring about change. Mana can move people. Teachers who reflect the quality of ihi, as well as the qualities of aroha and manaaki, are more likely to succeed in establishing effective relationships with students and in managing behaviour in the classroom (Macfarlane, cited in Fraser et al., 2005).

Mana (Macfarlane, 2004) and "withitness" (Kounin, 1977) have obvious similarities, and teachers who possess these qualities are more likely to establish control and structure within the classroom, providing a sense of stability and security. Determining one's own personal authoritative style can take time and practice. Personal authority is exemplified by a range of variables, including body language, tone of voice, attitudes and perceptions about personal and student matters. Teachers with mana and withitness portray the message that they are leaders.

Scenario example (adapted from Macfarlane, 2004): Maria

Maria, aged 14, has a reputation as a difficult-to-teach student. She is regularly involved in arguments with other students, and is known for being noncompliant on a number of occasions. She excels at sport, particularly netball. She arrives at school on a Monday morning eating a pie, and chooses to discard the paper bag on the ground. Here are three teacher responses:

Response one: Please pick up the paper, Maria.

Response two: Look here young lady, you know we have a rule in this school about litter. Pick up that paper bag now, or else! Do you hear me?

Response three: Maria, taihoa (wait a moment). The paper bag to the bin (pointing), thanks. Great netball result for the team on Saturday. Ka pai (good one).

The first response lacks assertiveness. Saying "please" as a lead in to the sentence is able to be interpreted as a plea from the teacher, allowing the balance of power to shift in favour of the student. There is perhaps a 50/50 chance that Maria may choose to comply. The second response is not assertive, it is aggressive. It is also threatening. It is not hard to imagine the tone with which the command was uttered. Or else what? Detention? Principal's office? On report? It ends with a trite question which allows Maria a right of reply. The tone and the tenor of Maria's reply might potentially elevate an already tentative situation to a level of intensity that both student and teacher may later regret, effectively closing the door on this student–teacher relationship (note the overlap to the previous element discussed, i.e., huakina mai). The odds that Maria will choose to comply in this instance are more likely to be 1 in 10.

The third response is both assertive and warm. Maria's name is used up front, denoting a matter-of-fact approach by the teacher. This teacher uses the pause and the gesture. It is highly likely that Maria will comply, regardless of the conversation around sport. However, the addendum relating to sport in this response demonstrates that the teacher knows the students and their interests. This teacher uses moderate language wisely. The third response is in line with the ihi element of the Hikairo Rationale; it is both assertive and warm. It is typical of a teacher who is capable of negotiating without difficulty and is skilled at avoiding conflict. It has a direct, crisp, and clear essence.

The next scenario outlines a teacher–student encounter that has the potential to turn into a highly charged and regrettable interaction.

Scenario example: Rory

Rory, a student at Railway School, is Māori and is physically bigger than his 13-year-old peers. Although he has been in trouble at school for aggressive and defiant behaviour toward students and teachers, it is now into Term Two and he appears to be more settled and is also making satisfactory progress generally. Angry outbursts do reappear at times. However, in the main his teacher, Mr MacEwan, maintains a good relationship with Rory.

One of the protocols in Mr MacEwan's class is a brief interchange at the beginning of the day, affectionately referred to by class members as "mihi in the morning" (see Macfarlane, 2004), during pastoral time before period one. This mihi includes an appropriate greeting: kia ora, mōrena, ata mārie, good morning. From the point of view of expressing aroha (common courtesy), this is very good practice. It is also good practice in terms of allowing the teacher to observe the āhua (attitude) of the students on their arrival. Many students regularly arrive at school feeling tired, hungry, angry, and/or upset. If this goes unnoticed, problems may well escalate as the day progresses. The ritual of the morning mihi may well prompt the teacher to get in early to address the situation, if necessary.

It does become necessary one Friday morning when Rory arrives at school and deliberately avoids contact with his teacher. Mr MacEwan senses that something untoward is going on. Let's take up the conversation from here:

> Mr MacEwan Kia ora, Rory. I notice I received no 'mihi' from you this morning?
>
> Rory   No, sir. Not in the mood.

The teacher detects a surliness, and he notices that Rory is wearing a scarf bearing distinctive markings. It is a school rule that gang regalia is not to be worn in any circumstances. It is important that the teacher addresses Rory's transgression of this rule. The particular markings on the scarf place both Rory and others at potential risk, given that they may be perceived as a direct challenge to some others. Mr MacEwan has to preserve a teacher–student relationship while bringing a very testing situation to order. Very tactfully, he remains calm, and then engages in a conversation about the school's dress code, all the time using a restrained tone. He notices Rory looks tired and quite disconsolate. Any number of factors may have contributed to this situation (taking care of siblings, late nights, substance abuse ...?); however, these are not the immediate priority. What matters is the here and now. After a rather one-way conversation, Mr MacEwan makes his next move:

> Mr MacEwan Okay Rory, you know the rule here. We've had a discussion. Time's marching on. I think you should hand me the scarf now.

For a few seconds (and that can be quite a long time in a situation like this), nothing happens. Mr MacEwan realises that the words he chose, and the rather casual way he posed the request, are not going to work. His approach was not as assertive as it needs to be for this potentially critical situation. Some weeks before, Mr MacEwan had put in place the fairness contract that was introduced in the previous Hikairo Rationale element, huakina mai. While reflecting on his rather weakly worded approach, Mr MacEwan remembers the fairness contract that exists between him and this student. He is then ready to make his next move:

> Mr MacEwan You have had a good year, Rory. Other teachers have commented on your progress and they like what they see. For the most part, I

	like what I see too. What I don't like is your behaviour at this time. We need to think about that. We need to think about the fact that you and I have a contract about being fair to each other. Tell me, have I been a fair teacher to you?
Rory	Yes, sir, I guess.
Mr MacEwan	Good. I think I have been. It's a two-way deal and I think that you have been fair to me too. But, given your attitude, and the thing with the scarf, I need to ask, are you being fair to me now?
Rory	Yes, sir, I guess.
Mr MacEwan	No, you are not being fair at this time. That is quite clear.

The teacher allows Rory time to process this last interchange. He senses that Rory is moved by the sharp reminder, and decides that it is now time to apply assertiveness, with a small measure of compromise:

> Mr MacEwan Rory, listen carefully to what I have got to say. Pass the scarf to me, now. Listen. Pass it to me now. And, I will look after it for you till after the last period. You can have it back then.

A sense of relief descends as Rory, in slow motion, reaches for the scarf around his neck, and hands it over to his teacher.

The strategies of taking up time and repeating the sentence (sometimes referred to as the cracked-record approach) paid off. Other strategies were also clearly effected in the final interchange. One was the implicit message from the teacher that the student should and could trust him to return the item of clothing at the end of the day. The teacher also put the student's name at the beginning of the sentence, whereas in the earlier request that was not the case.

Rory does not have the smoothest of passages throughout the rest of the day, but he makes it. Mr MacEwan, the astute practitioner, once again capitalises on his negotiation skills when he beckons Rory at the end of the day:

> Mr MacEwan It wasn't easy for you today, I know. But you made it, and full credit to you for that. Rory, I promised you that I would take care of this scarf for you and that you could have it back at the end of the day. Here it is. And don't wear it to school again. I need to make that clear.

Mr MacEwan has reiterated to the student that he is a teacher of integrity (he keeps his word) and the student is able to respond to that.

Note that this teacher's final sentence was not framed as a question that masked a challenge or threat. He did not say "Do I make that clear?" As an assertive teacher, Mr MacEwan closed the conversation with a statement that would be incisive, not tentative. The final eye contact between teacher and student is an agreeable one. They separate amicably.

There were a number of things that Mr MacEwan did not do. He did not admonish the student upon noticing that the school's dress code was being breached. Think about what may have transpired if another teacher (let's call him Mr Smart), had employed this approach:

Mr Smart   What do I see here young man? So you think that in this school there is one rule for you, and another for the rest of the school? Well, let me tell you that I have got news for you. Pass me that rag around your neck. We have a dress code here at this school, and it is 'instant confiscation'. I said pass me that . . .

Given some of the sensible assumptions that Mr MacEwan had made earlier about the mood that Rory was in that morning, along with some hunches about what might have contributed to his being in that mood, it would be fair to conclude that an interaction such as this between Mr Smart and Rory would have had a very different outcome. Their relationship would have been severely damaged, and when a relationship is damaged in such a way, it may take weeks or even months to rebuild—if indeed, it is able to be rebuilt at all. Mr Smart, it would seem, was not very smart in responding to this behavioural issue.

Grossman (2004) considers that almost everyone responds to someone who is being genuine. Teachers are being genuine when their words and actions express their true feelings and thoughts. When teachers are being genuine, it instils in their students a sense of trust and belief. Mr MacEwan was seen by Rory as being genuine because his words and actions expressed his feelings and thoughts—those of care, concern, understanding, and integrity.

Mr MacEwan adopted an authoritative approach to discipline. Teachers like Mr MacEwan tend to have an extremely effective management style. The students know the rules and the boundaries are clearly defined. The teacher is seen to be in charge, and students relate positively to the leadership and guidance that this provides. These teachers are cognisant of the dual functions that teachers transact in the classroom. While attending to the instructional function and the importance of the curriculum orientations, they are also attending to the managerial function that focuses on the processes of administering an orderly and well structured environment. The managerial function promotes order by way of procedures and rules, and by responding to disruptive behaviour (Doyle, 1986).

Increasingly, teachers are expressing concern about the impact of disruptive behaviours on learning and on classroom order, and how best to manage these. The Hikairo Rationale element of ihi suggests that an assertive approach, predicated on fairness and genuineness, offers teachers a range of strategies for promoting enhanced social interactions that will have positive implications for the behaviour and learning outcomes of students.

He toka tū moana
Arā he toa rongonui
Your strength is like a rock
That stands in raging waters

I runga i te manaaki: growing a caring community

In the Māori world, the concept of manaakitanga is expressed by showing respect, care, or kindness. This concept also means to entertain, to be hospitable and kind hosts to guests, to care for them (Williams, 1971). This is endorsed by Barlow (1993), who explains that the purpose of manaakitanga is to remind the host people that they should be kind to visitors who come to the marae. Barlow further states that "the most important attributes for the hosts are to provide an abundance of food, a place to rest, and to speak nicely to visitors so that peace prevails during the gathering" (p. 63). Ritchie (1992) describes manaakitanga as being reciprocal, unqualified caring. In the reciprocal sense, Ritchie adds that "there is simply faith that one day that which one has contributed will be returned" (p. 75) and that "you are obliged to support, to care for, be concerned about, to feed, shelter and nurture your kin, and especially when they are in need ... This is obligatory" (p. 78).

In terms of advancing these meanings into the domain of teaching and learning, manaakitanga is able to be interpreted in several ways. The first is that teachers need to facilitate a range of strategies that will promote the caring process in the classroom (the metaphor of providing an abundance of food). Secondly, classrooms need to be socially and culturally safe environments (the metaphor of providing a peaceful place). Thirdly, sound intercultural communication must prevail in the classroom (the metaphor of speaking nicely). Fourthly, manaakitanga is not optional, it is obligatory, and it has reciprocal ramifications, suggesting that teachers who value others will be valued in return (the metaphor of that which one has contributed being returned). There are obvious implications here for teachers who choose to disregard or underestimate the power of manaakitanga. Indeed, if intercultural communication and classroom effectiveness are to be strengthened, then the concept of manaakitanga needs to be embedded in the culture of the classroom.

Several national studies have indicated that New Zealand schools vary enormously in their effectiveness in managing for the achievement of education and socialisation outcomes for students who are Māori (Clark et al., 1996; Macfarlane, 2003; Reedy, 1992). Consequently, many Māori students who experience ongoing difficulties at school may not gain sufficient access to the social and academic skills necessary in order to participate successfully in contemporary New Zealand society. Teachers have a key role to play in building and maintaining equitable working relationships with students as well as in facilitating student learning and achievement. For teachers, this means having awareness, understanding, and experience in culturally responsive and inclusive teaching strategies (Moore et al., 1999; Wearmouth et al., 2005).

In a review of nine New Zealand studies, Macfarlane (2003) synthesised several key factors of culturally responsive teaching, offering guidance to teachers seeking to respond to the challenge of working effectively in diverse classrooms. These studies apportion varying degrees of emphasis on connections that exist between the behaviour of the student, and the quality of learning interactions and relationships needed for successful academic achievement. Schools, teachers, and their approaches to teaching vary enormously in terms of the quality of their interactions, and consequently in the learning outcomes that transpire for Māori and for other ethnic minority students.

The Hei Awhina Maatua programme (Glynn, Berryman, Atvars & Harawira, 1997) of the Poutama Pounamu Research Centre, the Te Kōtahitanga Ministry of Education project (Bishop, Berryman, Tiakiwai, & Richardson, 2003), and the AIMHI project co-ordinated by Hill and Hawk (2000) are examples of how culturally relevant pedagogy and successful learning outcomes are significantly linked. These studies demonstrate that connectedness, academic engagement, a supportive environment, and acknowledgment and recognition of difference are key qualities that make teaching and learning more meaningful for Māori students—and indeed for all students. Macfarlane (2002) studied three separate and successful educational sites within Te Arawa rohe (district): a traditional wānanga (place of learning), a secondary school classroom, and a primary school enrichment classroom. Across all three sites, he noted the central and critical role played by whānau in establishing and maintaining effective home, school, and community partnerships. Educators at all three sites were clearly "listening to culture" (Macfarlane, 2000). In addition, all sites evidenced a *context of care* for enhancing the overall wellbeing of their students.

The notion of a context of care is strongly portrayed within a report by Cooper, Arago-Kemp, Wylie, and Hodgen (2004). This report, *Te Rerenga ā te Pīrere* (The Flight of the Fledgling) is a longitudinal study of 111 kōhanga reo (language nests for early childhood) and kura kaupapa (primary school level) Māori students, and is one of the first in-depth research projects focusing on students in Māori medium settings. It reports widely on the educational and social environments, and on the students' learning.

This project tracks the development and progress of three cohorts of students, and is unique in that it reports on areas identified by those involved in the growth of kōhanga reo and kura kaupapa Māori as the most important features and goals. These include, for example, Māori language development, knowledge of tikanga Māori, and an emphasis on curriculum learning areas. In this study, students, parents, kaiako (teachers), and tumuaki (principals) were interviewed, and the students also completed a series of assessment tasks largely designed specifically for this project. Teaching te reo Māori me ona tikanga (language and culture) in a safe environment, and the development of a strong sense of pride and identity, were perceived to be the main philosophies of the kōhanga reo and kura involved. These philosophies were also cited as the main reasons that parents chose this model of provision of education for their children. It was of key importance to parents that the education being provided was whānau oriented.

It is crucial to note here that today, as in the past, manaakitanga remains one of the compelling forces that supports the development of effective curriculum and pedagogy for Māori. Effective curriculum and pedagogy for Māori are likely to be found in culturally safe learning environments, where both the teacher and students engage in a reciprocal relationship of respect and understanding for and about one another (Macfarlane et al., 2005). In the classroom, the context of care can be demonstrated through providing support and nurturing (Noddings, 2002), having high expectations of all students, and creating a culturally affirming learning environment (Bateman, 2007; Gay, 2000; Macfarlane, 2004).

Two ethnographic studies, one in a school in the United States, and one in a school in the Waikato region, which were carried out by Cavanagh (2003, 2005), also illustrate the importance of providing caring contexts for students. Both studies demonstrated that culturally safe classrooms encouraged strong family input, fostered reciprocal learning between students and teachers, and employed culturally grounded pedagogies such as: interchanging the roles of teacher and learner (the concept of ako); scaffolded tutoring, where more skilled students took responsibility for teaching less skilled students (the concept of tuakana-teina); and a constructivist approach to curriculum delivery.

Constructivist approaches involve collaboration between teachers and students, within an holistic perspective based on collective learning, shared responsibility and ownership of learning activities (Bishop et al., 2002), and on authentic, place-based learning (Penetito, 2004). In constructivist classrooms, meaningful learning takes place because teachers adopt a position that regards students as autonomous and responsible learners. Teachers in these classrooms also: provide students with opportunities for doing things differently; respect their students' creativity; and co-construct with their students a learning environment where students are allowed to be who and what they are (Macfarlane, Glynn, Grace, & Penetito, 2005).

The Hikairo Rationale element, i runga i te manaaki, is directly linked to empathetic people taking on the perspective of "feeling with" rather than "feeling for" an individual. McAllister and Irvine (2002) comment on how an empathetic disposition often manifests itself in teachers' caring relationships with students:

> Researchers have noted that students, especially students of color, who have caring relationships with their teachers are more motivated and perform better academically than students who do not (Foster, 1995; Gay, 2000; Irvine, 1990). In addition, empathy can potentially foster openness, attentiveness, and positive relationships. In culturally diverse classrooms, being open and flexible helps teachers adjust to varying contexts (Delpit, 1995). Teachers are better able to modify pedagogy and curricula to fit their students' needs . . . (p. 434)

It is easier for students to relate to and to like an empathetic teacher. These teachers are liked by students because they express their manaakitanga in many different forms, some of which include active listening, patience, openmindedness, strategically attending to students, and having a sense of humour.

Active listening involves encouraging students to communicate things that concern them, providing sound feedback, and checking for meaning.

Patience involves the temporary acceptance of unacceptable or low-level behaviour. This is an appropriate strategy for students who struggle to contain or manage all their behaviour all the time. Sometimes their impulsivity means that a misbehaviour will recur. Teachers should be patient, within reason, by allowing sufficient time for the student to self-manage, or by adopting a technique that will address the misbehaviour with a low-level response.

Openmindedness is the antithesis of the zero tolerance approach. When teachers accept that some student behaviours are far harder to change than others, they look deeper into possible physiological or psychological causes, and adapt techniques or seek more specialised assistance.

Attending to students involves acknowledging students' positive behaviour, and paying less attention to negative behaviour. Choosing appropriate rewards and a suitable system for their delivery are often the most difficult aspects of behaviour management in the classroom. According to Smith and Laslett (1993, p. 102), helpful techniques include "token economy" for groups and "contingency contracting" for individuals.

Humour is appreciated by students. Teachers who are too serious, too often, do little to engender appreciation in students. It is important that humour be light and amiable, not based on sarcasm or put-down.

I runga i te manaaki is portrayed as the arteries in the trunk of the tree that extend outward to the branches (see Figure 7.2), emphasising the all-pervading nature of caring. The element of care is something that is vibrant in the learning environment when empathy is experienced by students, and demonstrated in the actions and feelings of the teacher. Teachers who genuinely care for their students, their learning environments, and themselves are generally liked by students and their colleagues. Grossman (2004) contends that students who like their teachers learn more and behave better than students who do not. Students are more likely to have positive feelings toward teachers who listen to them and encourage them to express their feelings.

It should be noted that while manaakitanga is an obligatory requirement for becoming a culturally responsive teacher, or even an effective teacher in diverse settings, on its own it is not sufficient. Teachers must also know their subject matter well, and be technically competent in all areas of classroom systems and management. McAllister and Irvine (2002) assert that the existence of this tension should not dissuade teacher-education and professional-development programmes from promoting the conviction that an empathetic disposition is a desirable trait.

> *Manaakitia te tangata, ahakoa ko wai, ahakoa nō hea*
> Treat people respectfully, irrespective of who they are
> or where they come from

Rangatiratanga: motivating learners

Holding and exercising status within an event or environment is a central meaning of the Hikairo Rationale element of rangatiratanga. Applicable to everyone, rangatiratanga, according to Ritchie (1992), "is related to effectiveness, to being good at things or getting things done . . . it may refer to drawing an additional boost of power, of strength, of mana" (p. 70).

There is little doubt that rangatiratanga is linked to the concept of mana. Barlow (1993) explains that in modern times, the term *mana* has taken on various meanings, including the power of gods, ancestors, land, and individuals (mana atua, mana tipuna, mana whenua, mana tangata). For the purposes of education, mana tangata or mana motuhake appears a most appropriate complementary factor to the concept of rangatiratanga. Barlow elaborates that mana tangata "is the power acquired by an individual according to his or her ability and effort to develop skills and gain knowledge in particular areas" (p. 62). Macfarlane (2004) links rangatiratanga status to exceptional classroom practice, and to a term coined by Kounin (1977), that of withitness. Macfarlane proposes that withitness is a factor that differentiates effective teachers from ineffective teachers. Effective teachers have a range of strategies in their classroom management toolkit that they implement skilfully when required. *Kia Hiwa Rā! Listen to Culture—Māori Students' Plea to Educators* (Macfarlane, 2004) is an additional text that describes the following strategies in more detail:

- scanning the room
- making eye contact
- working the crowd
- getting physical proximity
- using body language

- speaking in a student-friendly vernacular
- emanating an enthusiasm that ripples out to others
- giving whole-class rewards (p. 87)
- carrying out individual or class projects that build social bonds, e.g., the Treaty of Waitangi in early February (p. 88)
- facilitating a whole-school approach to learning, e.g., "te wiki o te reo Māori". (pp. 92–93)

While some of these strategies can empower and encourage students by focusing them on their learning, redirecting their attention, and addressing behaviour difficulties, there is a limit to how frequently they should be implemented by the teacher. Too much, too often leads to satiation, at which point the intervention strategy is liable to become less effective.

An argument for instilling and fostering self-motivation in students has merit. Cultivating personal qualities of motivation can give students resources for developing aspiration, achieving goals, becoming independent learners, and fostering resilience in the face of setbacks. The development of resiliency is described by Stanley (2006) as the ability of the student to bounce back successfully, despite their socialisation in adverse circumstances.

According to Alderman (1999) a central theme in contemporary motivation theories and literature is the focus on self-regulated learners. These learners have what is known as volition, or strength of will to persist. Newmann (1992) describes the teacher's role as one of engaging students in the hard work of the school: the ongoing cycle of reading for meaning, completing assigned studies, correcting errors, and starting over again. Mitchell and Mitchell (1998) studied 40 Māori students who gained high scores in School Certificate English and mathematics. They showed that student (and teacher) motivation was seen as a critical factor and several themes emerged from the students' voices:

> I'm efficient . . . I like high marks . . . I always attend any extra tuition offered . . . I want to get a good job . . . One teacher helped me keep going . . . (pp. 49–50)

While these students received a lot of encouragement from their parents, and had innate ability, they also worked hard and were competitive; they attempted to complete tasks and to make the completed work the best that it could be. These students had learnt to be motivated about their approach to their education. Moreover, they recalled teachers who had high expectations of them, and who "pushed them".

This study also referred to several Māori students who had not gone on to tertiary education. These students reported on negative experiences with teachers at school. The message here is profound and unfortunate: the actions of some teachers may actually hinder or halt students' progress at school. Clearly, however, many teachers possess the qualities of rangatiratanga, and inspire their students to persevere and forge ahead toward their educational goals. The following descriptions of rangatiratanga come from two paraprofessionals talking about the lead teacher in their classroom:

> She places importance of boosting the success of Māori children. She wants our tamariki (children) to understand the importance of learning and to never forget who they are, and where they come from, and how far they can go.
>
> Brilliant. She has the children eating out of the palm of her hand. She has taught us all so much in such a short space of time.
>
> She is a role model; interesting and captivating. She knows what she is talking about. The children develop high self-esteem in a relatively short span of time. And they maintain that esteem in other contexts.
>
> (Macfarlane, 2003, p. 179)

One must be cautious not to perceive the notion of the self-regulated learner as the child as a "lone scientist". A case must be made for ongoing social influences in emergent interaction within the instructional environment. The potential of co-regulation within Vygotsky's (1978) zone of proximal development for understanding student motivation includes the power of peer participation in curriculum tasks. Co-operative learning strategies suggest effective ways of addressing learning where students engage individually, while also drawing from the value of collective responsibility.

Co-operative learning is "a generic term for the instructional organisation of children into mixed ability study groups in which participants cooperate with one another to achieve academic goals" (Rich, cited in Winzer & Mazurek, 1998, p. 302). Within these groups, the attainment of goals is realised through full and active participation of peers in the activities.

Brown and Thomson (2000) declare that co-operative learning contexts are able to enhance both academic and social skills, by providing structures that allow effective learning strategies to develop. Further, Brown and Thomson query how essential social skills are able to be learnt well *without* a co-operative group structure. Medcalf (1995) outlines the two key components of co-operative learning essential for achievement gains: first, group rewards are contingent on all members reaching either individual or collective goals; secondly, individual accountability to the group is necessary. These components provide incentives for students to work together and communicate effectively. Because co-operative learning combines academic and social skills, its symbiotic nature is able to be further highlighted. The process ensures that enhanced learning results from, and is reliant on, social skills and respectful interactions. These in turn are enhanced because of greater academic gains (Bateman, 2007).

Ongoing research into classroom practice clearly indicates that co-operative learning is advantageous for all students, not just those with special learning and teaching needs (Brown & Thomson, 2000; Fuchs & Fuchs, 1994; Good & Brophy, 1994; Johnson, Johnson, & Maruyama, 1983). It is also clear that co-operative learning contexts are advantageous to Māori students, because they include the social concept of ako, which recognises the concurrent and reciprocal nature of teaching and learning (Macfarlane & Glynn, cited in Brown & Thomson, 2000). Tuakana status (the status of senior students) and kaiārahitanga (leadership) qualities are shown in co-operative learning by what Metge (1983) refers to as "modelling" or "learning through exposure" and "learning in groups". Kapahaka (rhythmical dance) is also a form of co-operative learning. In the kapahaka learning paradigm, new members are placed among more experienced members until they too obtain mastery. Moreover, contributing to group process is as important as achieving the group goals.

Co-operative learning in the classroom, however, is also a way of bringing about crossethnic socialisation. Johnson et al. (1983) contend that when children from diverse backgrounds work co-operatively together, the status of group members tends to be equalised, with all members developing personal regard and respect for one another.

It needs to be borne in mind that co-operative learning is a structured process, sometimes intricate in nature. Therefore, in the first instance, co-operative skills have to be taught. Subsequently, details such as room arrangement, student placement, and evaluation of learning performance have to be seriously considered. Further modification of one or two strategies may be necessary for the involvement of Māori students. For example, face-to-face active interaction may have the potential to present itself as a little too in-your-face. Māori students may be more responsive to a "kānohi ki te kānohi" approach to this strategy. Graham (2003) describes kānohi ki te kānohi as a trusting and sharing approach, wherein each other's credibility is nurtured. Explanations surrounding this Māori perception of connecting would be fitting, as it would present co-operative learning as nonthreatening in its structure. Māori students, in the main, prefer a co-operative orientation towards learning and life, and the motivational aspects within co-operative learning classroom structures have the potential to facilitate improved academic engagement (Macfarlane, 2004).

The most important motivational outcome of co-operative learning is the effect on student self-esteem. This method brings about a feeling of being liked and included by peers, and advances a feeling of academic competence:

> The motivation of low-achieving students, in particular, can be enhanced or inhibited by the type of goal structure. If the structure is competitive, low-achieving students will perceive that they lack ability in comparison with their more successful classmates. Low achievers should experience greater success in co-operative classrooms because co-operative group structures tend to minimize the focus on ability (Ames & Ames, 1984). More important, co-operative goal structures can foster peer norms for higher achievement. (Slavin, cited in Alderman, 1999, p. 188)

All teachers are able to recognise classes where students are highly motivated. There is a vitality about them, as in the classroom of Year 2 Māori children described below:

> The room had a 'texture' which incorporated real sight, sound, smell, and taste. Importantly, the students seemed to delight in being there, in the presence of a skilled practitioner, who valued each of them for simply being who they were. Children reputed to have behaviour problems did not misbehave. Most were said to have learning difficulties, yet in this environment they were motivated to achieve better, and records of their progress attested to that. So-called withdrawn children became vocal contributors, and impulsive children seemed more in control of themselves. (Macfarlane, 2004, pp. 28–29)

McInerney and McInerney (1998) add that these types of environments are those where teacher and students work harmoniously and energetically, and are task-oriented contexts. They also explain that within any class there is a great variation among individuals in terms of the level of motivation for particular tasks. Levels of motivation apply to teachers as well as students. Motivation of students whose skills or abilities are less well developed will require greater guidance and direction from the teacher. Alderman (1999) contends that this may require the teacher to use structure, including the stating of clear goals and directions, with frequent monitoring, feedback, and opportunities to taste success. In line with Vygotsky's (1978) zone of proximal development, as students become more able to guide and motivate themselves, the teacher is gradually able to reduce the level of support. As students progress to higher levels of self-management and motivation, they are more strongly positioned to set their own goals and persist in the face of adversity.

> *Tama tū, tama ora*
> *Tama noho, tama mate*
> One who stands, thrives
> One who sits, withers

Kōtahitanga: linking home and school

The Hikairo Rationale element of kōtahitanga can mean different things to different people. One acceptable connotation is that kōtahitanga is concerned with the process of linking, of seeking unity, and of achieving a sense of togetherness. Ritchie (1992) describes kōtahitanga as the Māori political process where consensus is achieved through discussion. By this process, people are brought together so that all personal differences and opinions are aired. Even if all opinions cannot be incorporated into the final decision, they are all given due respect, because of the mana of the persons who hold these opinions.

On a wider scale, kōtahitanga can be viewed as the means of establishing a communication process toward the respectful coexistence of two historic cultures. This involves building links, and not assuming that difference does not exist. Ritchie (1992) portrays kōtahitanga as being the bridge for cultural understanding and communication:

> It is only as we start to examine, recognise and attend to the construction of the inter-culture that we can become secure with biculturalism, which does not, and need not, divide us. Separate we will need to be, perhaps more often in the future than in the recent past as respect and awareness grow, but there is no necessity for division. Kōtahitanga is, or can be, a bridge for both cultures. (p. 96)

In the context of education, neither home nor school can operate to the optimum in isolation. Home and school must work together if a healthy climate for learning is to be provided and sustained for young people. Often, a school will develop positive learning environments and experiences for its students, only to observe a lack of interest or support from the home. Alternatively, sometimes the home will display high levels of enthusiasm and interest, only to observe these being responded to with indifference by the classroom teacher or school.

How to develop and maintain meaningful and effective relationships between parents, family members, and educational professionals is a subject that has received widespread attention in the literature and in educational conferences, educational agencies, and school staffrooms throughout the country. However, Simpson (1996) considers that, in spite of such attention, educators and other professionals involved with students with special needs are regularly ill at ease and ineffectual when attempting to engage, communicate, and collaborate with parents and family members. Fine (1989) adds that even those professionals with expertise in direct service to children and youth, and who are also proficient in relating to other professional disciplines, often find it difficult to link and engage with parents and family. When culture is added to the mix, linking and developing relationships with whānau becomes an even greater challenge for many educators.

In a recent project carried out by Bevan-Brown (2005), information was gathered about the scope, prevalence, and effectiveness of programmes and services for Māori children and youth with special needs. This study found that the involvement of parents, whānau, and the Māori community was a significant factor when it came to making a difference for these young people. Durie (1994), Macfarlane et al. (2005), Pere (1991), and a host of other researchers consider whānau to be a central component in their respective models for health and education:

> . . . the family is the prime support system for Māori, providing care and nurturance, not only in physical terms, but culturally and emotionally. (Durie, 1994, p. 73)

> . . . it is the process of treating people as if they were kin. It involves the central importance of establishing and maintaining effective and equitable relationships between teachers and learners. (Macfarlane et al., 2005, p. 34)

Bevan-Brown's (2005) study found that such views about the importance of whānau were widely accepted and promoted by many service providers. However, the analyses also revealed that many different challenges are faced by people and organisations providing services and programmes for Māori learners with special needs. One significant revelation was that Māori parents were reluctant to participate in the survey, as they were too shy to make their needs known or to complain about poor-quality service provisions. While

Bevan-Brown's survey showed that a wide range of provisions existed for Māori students and their whānau, bicultural training for all staff in both mainstream and Māori services needs to be developed:

> It is argued that pre-service and in-service education should include a substantial, compulsory Māori component. Bicultural training would not only increase workers' cultural competence but, hopefully, it would also help to change those Pākehā-centric beliefs and attitudes which, at present, work against the accommodation and valuing of Māori concepts and ways of working. To bring about this attitudinal change, the bicultural curriculum would need to include a critical examination of majority cultural influence in education and society and an in-depth consideration of the causes, impact and maintenance of unequal power relationships, prejudice, racism, disabilism, social injustice, inequality and poverty. Along with compulsory bicultural training, measures should be introduced to increase special educational expertise among people involved in Māori organisations and Māori-medium education. (Bevan-Brown, 2005, p. 9)

Educational underachievement of many Māori students in mainstream schools has been attributed to a number of sources. Some Māori grandparents retain the memory of their own schooling, in which they were forbidden to use their own language (Walker, 1991) and were put down as an inferior society practising an inferior culture. Some of the children of these grandparents are now themselves parents, and have little language or cultural knowledge that is Māori to pass on to their own children. These experiences can be compared with the plight of some first nations' Americans who descended from several generations of a semi-assimilated minority and whose sense of loss translated into a deep suspicion on their part of the majority culture's professional agencies and schools (Kallam, Hoernicke, & Coser, 1994).

A lack of understanding of Māori customs on the part of the dominant New Zealand culture may be one critical reason why many Māori students fail to achieve in mainstream educational settings, and are regularly excluded from them. In a society which is frequently described as bicultural or multicultural, it is not surprising that individual underachievement is often explained by reference to perceived deficits within the individual's cultural background. However, it is increasingly common to hear the contention that "the style of content of service delivery in such areas as health, social welfare, and education should be constructed so as to take account of the cultural background of the people receiving these services, or that the service should be culturally appropriate" (Morrisey, 1997, p. 93). This suggests that professionals need to

consider either facilitating workshops (if they are the experienced party) or attending workshops (if they are the less experienced party) selected from the following options:
- early history of New Zealand
- the Treaty of Waitangi
- the Māori renaissance
- understanding tikanga Māori
- understanding Te Ao Māori.

Further exposure to basic but essential aspects of Māoritanga will not solve everything, but it will begin to grow professionals' awareness and cultural sensitivity, which are prerequisites to the development of effective relationships with parents (henceforth intended to include caregivers), and whānau. Education professionals are advised to learn the history of their school and its surrounds. Often this requires going to the people themselves, to listen and to talk with them, and work amongst them in their own environment. There will be times when some things will be difficult to understand. Honesty is the best policy in these instances. A comment such as, "I don't understand, and I need help with this" will most likely result in help being provided.

Despite the challenges associated with building partnerships with parents and whānau of culturally diverse learners with particular education needs, such partnerships can be developed. Shea and Bauer (1991) propose that among the most significant of these strategies is building an atmosphere of respect, as the basis for the kind of coequal relationship that is most conducive to effective collaboration. The following are suggestions for developing an atmosphere of respect between teachers, professionals, and parents/whānau (adapted from Midgette, cited in Ford, Obiakor, & Patton, 1995):

- Use appropriate titles: Depending on the context, the use of appropriate titles, such as whaea and matua, kuia or koro, may be adopted.
- Use the appropriate tone of voice: Speak assuredly and with courtesy and respect.
- Use understandable vernacular: For many parents, acronyms such as RTLB, GSE, MoE, SSS, might not mean a great deal. Do not be overly sophisticated, but remember also never to be condescending.
- Maintain honesty: Give accurate answers to questions, and follow up any promises.
- Include parents' views: Include their views in reports and assure parents

that their views will be included in any decision making concerning their son or daughter.

In talking with parents and whānau, it is important to assure them that what they share about their child and about their whānau will help teachers and consultants to understand their child better, and that their contribution is valued and welcomed. What parents and whānau communicate helps the professional educator to glean invaluable information about the experiences students have had at home and in the community, as well as some of the attitudes and feelings that the parents and whānau have toward their children. There will also be times in the consultation process when parents and whānau will contribute with genuine trepidation. Many still harbour the feeling from their own school days that an interview with a teacher always means something bad has happened—or is about to happen.

Parents and whānau thrive on praise and encouragement, as we all do. Consequently, interactions with parents and whānau tend to be more productive if conversations start with a child's strengths rather than perceived weaknesses, as each youngster, without exception, has strengths. Jenkins (1961) and Macfarlane (2003) contend that parents and whānau are quick to sense the feelings and attitudes of the professional toward their child, and toward them. Parents and whānau respond to the teacher who is comfortable and natural, whose genuine interest in their child and whānau makes them feel that, "Here is someone with whom I can talk about my child—about what pleases me and about what concerns me."

The benefits for students when effective relationships are formed with parents, caregivers, and whānau are considerable. They include improved learning, attendance, and morale, and decreased underachievement, low self-esteem, and truancy (Ramsay, Hawk, Harold, Marriott, & Poskitt, 1993). Fraser (in Fraser et al., 2005) adds that even those educational professionals who are a little hesitant about engaging with parents and whānau do concede that collaboration between the home and the school does benefit the school.

In order to reap the benefits, schools need to take the time to foster the necessary dialogue with parents and whānau. In collaborating with Māori families, there are often concerns over whom to consult, the appropriate use of protocol, and governance arrangements; these need to be worked through as the relationship develops. The Ministry of Education (2000) has provided a range of guidelines for boards of trustees and schools on engaging with Māori parents, whānau, and communities. Although these guidelines do not focus specifically on parents of students with learning and behaviour difficulties, their suggestions are particularly useful for schools and professionals to develop a more inclusive relationship with Māori parents, whānau, and communities. Indeed, the guidelines include a section on "School activities and interaction with Māori parents", and outline some ways to increase Māori parents' participation. Interestingly, but not surprisingly, many of the examples are relevant to all parents. Their suggestions include:

- be whānau friendly
- use the school's resources to enhance Māori parents' learning
- organise social activities that will encourage Māori parents into the school
- find practical ways to assist Māori parents to get to meetings
- identify the skills of Māori parents and whānau
- improve the means by which information is provided to Māori whānau
- look for appropriate opportunities to attend tangi and hui
- consult with local tangata whenua
- allow the community to access school facilities
- obtain business sponsorship
- develop community and iwi networks.

The final guideline, that of developing networks, warrants some elaboration. The Ministry of Education (2000) reported on several schools deriving great benefit from setting up networks in the community with other organisations with which they have regular consultation. These included kōhanga reo, marae committees, iwi social services, Maatua Whāngai, Māori Wardens Association, iwi health providers, and kaumātua. Networks with other Māori organisations, sports clubs, and kapahaka groups also encouraged Māori parents to become involved and take part in gala days and wānanga, where Māori took leadership roles.

No resource has the capacity to impede successful collaboration more than time. Finding adequate time to deal with the day-to-day responsibilities of curriculum and programme planning in both general and special education is difficult enough in itself; time demands over and above that can present an arduous challenge. Bos and Vaughn (1998) assert that if time is not built into teachers' schedules, collaboration is simply unlikely to occur on a regular basis. Furthermore, if it is not part of the work schedule, then teachers may resent having to collaborate, because it not only takes time away from their regular professional schedules, but impinges on their personal schedules as well.

Professional assistance

In New Zealand, professional groups exist to help teachers and schools in responding to students who present with challenging behaviours. Resource Teachers: Learning and Behaviour (RTLB) are involved mainly in working, inclusively and ecologically, alongside teachers who have referred a student with moderate learning and/or behavioural needs. Group Special Education (GSE) personnel are involved in working with students who present with severe behavioural needs. Both the RTLB professional development training consortium and the GSE Māori strategy draw from a noted Tainui whakataukī when explaining the multiple pathways that support the process of collaboration with teachers, parents, and the community:

Kōtahi te kōhao o te ngira	There is but one eye of the needle
E kuhuna ai	Through which passes
Te miro pango	The black thread
Te miro mā	The white thread
Te miro whero	And the red thread

Drawing on this concept, Kana and Harawira (cited in Fraser et al., 1995) proposed a set of principles upon which the GSE has designed an inclusive approach toward special education provision in Aotearoa. This approach incorporates three strands:

Te miro pango is the strand that relates to Māori working with Māori, where the early point of contact for the Māori child is a Māori staff member or helper.

Te miro mā relates to non-Māori working in appropriate ways with Māori students and their whānau. This will occur after guidance and training have been provided.

Te miro whero is essentially Māori and non-Māori professionals working together to enhance the success of the student. Properly administered, this red strand has the potential to lead to the development of more culturally appropriate approaches to student interventions, and more wholesome outcomes.

The RTLB service is itinerant, so every school has access to one or more RTLB. These experienced teachers are specially trained to work with teachers and principals, parents and caregivers, family, whānau, and community members to support positive outcomes for students. Nationally, approximately 50 RTLB work specifically with Māori students. The work of RTLB involves assessing a student's needs within an ecological framework, and developing learning programmes to overcome any difficulties. They work with individual students, groups, whole classes, and with whole school systems.

Training for professionals—RTLB, special education advisers, psychologists—focuses on skills in relationship building, communication, and collaboration. Additionally, the training helps professionals understand the complex nature of families' infrastructure and ways of viewing the world. According to Darling (cited in Hardman et al., 1999), good training encourages practitioners to be reflective, that is, to take a look at their own attitudes, values, and beliefs about families with young people with learning and behaviour difficulties. Good training also impresses on practitioners the need to view parents and whānau as partners in a team rather than being the source of the student's problem.

Another successful initiative, the Home–School Partnership Training Programme has been facilitated by the Ministry of Education in more than 124 schools across New Zealand. Initially, the programme was devised to support Pasifika parents where English was their second language, but its effectiveness indicated that a wider range of parent communities found the training useful. It was then broadened to include parents from all ethnicities. The regional School Support Services advisers ran the project as part of their core work. Their role in supporting schools with this programme is based on the principle of schools involving parents in their community, so that they can become more involved in their children's learning. The kaupapa (philosophy) of the Home–School Partnership Training Programme is founded on cultural inclusion and genuine partnerships in school (Ministry of Education, 2003). This project's philosophy (along with others mentioned in this section) is a fine example of the dynamics of kōtahitanga coming into play; building a bridge between home and school.

Essentially, kōtahitanga embellishes unity and bonding. These collaborative practices were fundamental to tipuna. Traditionally, Māori lived in close-knit communities, worked together, and planted food together. Everybody contributed to the wellbeing of the tribe. "One of the reasons for unity was to give everyone an equal share of the resources so that no one suffered unduly... The concept of unity pervaded every aspect of tribal functions and activities" (Barlow, 1993, p. 57). Ritchie (1992) describes kōtahitanga as the process of becoming one out of many. It is the process of recognising everyone's mana, and of bringing a sense of unity to a specific context (for example, whānau, parish, school, classroom).

The process of reaching consensus is not simple, and it can be of considerable duration. Many hapū and iwi have records of arguments and tensions in their distant and recent histories (Macfarlane, 2004). But through reason, understanding, and perseverance, compromise will prevail over contention.

> *Nāu te rourou*
> *Nāku te rourou*
> *Ka ora ai te iwi*
> With your food basket
> And my food basket
> There will be ample

Awhinatia: toward restorative practice

"Lifeline for students no schools want" said a *Waikato Times* headline on 13 January 2000. The article referred to teenagers who had a lot in common: "Almost all of them have been suspended more than once, and some of them simply never bothered enrolling at secondary school after they were expelled from primary school. Most of them hate school" (*Waikato This Week*, 2000, p. 21). Many students such as these are at risk of ending up on the streets and of ruining their chances of a happy and successful life. Some of them, however, are caught in the last safety net that the education system can offer them: alternative education in an on-site or off-site centre. A paradox to inclusion this might well be; a reality it most certainly is.

The concern about the numbers of students being turned away from school, or turned off school, has not escaped the Ministry of Education, which encourages schools to use the ultimate sanctions of stand-down and suspension as infrequently as possible. Some regions are reported to be making significant reductions in their stand-downs and suspension rates. The Suspension Reduction Initiative (SRI) has assisted many schools to increase engagement and reduce unacceptable student behaviour that leads to students being excluded. Stand-downs and suspensions are continuing to reduce in most schools that are part of the SRI project, indicating that sustainability is being achieved (Ministry of Education, 2005) and that the concerns for students at risk are being responded to. The Ministry of Education's Statement of Intent 2006–2011 centred on its mission statement, "To Raise Achievement and Reduce Disparity" (Ministry of Education, 2006a). The Statement incorporates three vital factors focused on increasing student engagement: effective teaching, family and community engagement, and quality providers. The Statement proposes that increased student engagement in the learning process is undoubtedly linked to better learning outcomes for students.

The principles and elements of the Hikairo Rationale concur with this. However, not all students succeed. The term *at-risk* can be defined in many different ways. Using education as a frame of reference, Smith et al. (2004) define at-risk children and youth as "those who are in situations that can lead to academic, personal, and behavioural problems that could limit their success in school and later in life" (p. 386). Many factors place students at risk of failure at school, including poverty, parental neglect, substance abuse, learning difficulties, and negative peer influence. Smith and his colleagues warn that although the presence of one or more of these factors may make failure more likely for students, it is important not to associate children who are living with poverty, for example, with at-risk status, as many do well at school. Others, like the three students in the case study below, clearly need help.

Restorative justice: Pae, Dean, and Matt

Two university lecturers, one non-Māori and one Māori, and both former secondary school teachers, were asked to facilitate a restorative conference for three Māori boys—Pae, Dean, and Matt—at a provincial secondary school. Both lecturers had been involved in the Ministry of Education's Restorative Conferencing in Schools Trial in 1999–2000, and also in the Ministry of Education's Suspension Reduction Initiative (SRI).

Together they had discussed the meaning of restorative justice in broad terms, as well as in more culturally specific terms. In broad terms, they considered that restorative justice constitutes an innovative approach to offending and inappropriate behaviour; it places repairing the harm done to relationships between people over and above the need to apportion or assign blame and dispense punishment. According to Hopkins (2004), a restorative approach in a school shifts the emphasis from managing behaviour to focusing on the building, nurturing, and repairing of relationships. This is a far cry from many traditional responses to conflicts between students, or to unacceptable behaviour. Those responses sought to find out what happened, who was to blame, and what was to be the appropriate response to deter and possibly punish those at fault, so that the behaviour would not be repeated.

The approach proposed by Hopkins is in tandem with traditional Māori disciplinary procedures, and with Judge Michael Brown's "model of healing" (see Macfarlane, in Fraser et al., 2005, p. 109). This approach is also compatible with a culturally specific approach.

Culture constitutes an extremely important component in student conferences. People from one ethnic background are likely to enter a conferencing situation with very different views and expectations from those who come from another background. Conferencing is not new to Māori people. Traditional Māori societies had this down to a fine art and many examples are manifested magnificently in mythology, legends, and history. Contemporary Māori society has retained an abundance of what tipuna (ancestors) had to offer, despite the infiltration of Western processes on conferencing techniques. For Māori, oneness of tinana, hinengaro, and wairua is often perceived as a distinction from the rationality and logic that influence thinking from a Western perspective (Fraser, 2004). If the conferencing process is going to be of value to Māori rangatahi (youth) who find themselves in trouble at school, and at risk of being excluded from it, then it needs to embrace Māori philosophy and logic (O'Connor & Macfarlane, 2002).

Four quintessential features illustrating pre-European Māori discipline are identified by Olsen, Maxwell, and Morris (cited in McElrea, 1994). They are:

1. an emphasis on reaching *consensus* and involving the whole community
2. a desired outcome of *reconciliation* and a settlement acceptable to all parties, rather than the isolation and punishment of the offender
3. not to apportion blame, but to *examine* the wider reason for the wrong, with an implicit assumption that there was often wrong on both sides
4. less concern with whether or not there had been a breach of law, and more concern with the *restoration* of harmony. (p. 8)

These traditional Māori disciplinary procedures continue to feature in contemporary Māori society, and are in tandem with the restorative justice approach (itself ancient in its origins) to conflict resolution in the area of youth offending.

James Ritchie (1992) refers to the complexities, difficulties, and intrigue that are encountered by Māori in their endeavour to reach consensus. If consensus is to be achieved through discussion, then it is to the hui process that many Māori people turn (Macfarlane, cited in Fraser et al., 2005). A unit of study in the RTLB curriculum (Macfarlane, 2001) refers to this process as Te Hui Whakatika, which means "meeting together to put an issue to right". The four broad principles of *consensus, reconciliation, examination,* and *restoration* are critical to an effective school conference, or hui.

Pae, Dean, and Matt had been referred to attend a Hui Whakatika so that a group of people could collectively address what was considered to be a critical situation for these students. The deputy principal (DP) had referred the boys because of their severe and challenging behaviours. These included verbally abusing teachers, truancy, and bullying other students by the use of intimidation and standover tactics. They were not willing to share their thoughts or feelings about their behaviours, and the school counsellors' attempts to guide and support them had achieved little. Outside school, their activities had also been unsatisfactory and the police had become involved. These young men were in crisis.

The facilitators advised the DP that the conventional phases to the restorative practice process would apply, and that he was to carry these out accordingly. The first of these phases is the pre-hui meetings. These involve:
- meeting with the boys and their whānau
- meeting with any students who had been affected
- hearing the stories of what had happened
- preparing people for what will happen at the hui
- establishing a willingness on the part of the boys to make amends
- explaining the process
- selecting a venue and time.

The DP was advised to take a Māori colleague with him to guide the application of protocol and, where necessary and appropriate, augment the making of connections with individuals and whānau. Prior to the hui itself, separate meetings took place with the students, their whānau, and others who were affected by the behaviour of Pae, Dean, and Matt. These meetings were called to explain the process and to gather some information. The teachers involved were also consulted early in the process. The meeting with the teachers was to explain the process and their role in the subsequent hui. Once the early meetings had been completed, the participants were then invited to the hui to help the three boys, their whānau, and the school.

The DP invested a tremendous amount of commitment and energy in the pre-hui phase. He was able to convince a significant number of key people—parents, teachers, the teacher aide—of the importance of the meeting, and was able to secure their resolve to attend. He even made transport arrangements so that one whānau was able to be present.

Preparing the ground for hui of this kind appears more complex than it actually is. It is, however, important that the pre-hui tasks be carried out thoroughly, all the time being respectful of the mana of each person, and honouring their choice about the part that each would play. People need to be prepared for what will happen at the hui, as well as receiving an explanation of the process. If these details are not attended to, participants run the risk of "going in cold", and in those circumstances are more likely to withdraw and not contribute as freely as they might like to.

It is important also that the student be willing to make amends. So important, in fact, that if the student is not willing to make amends, the hui does not proceed. This does not mean the end of the road; it means that another conversation with the student will have to take place at another time. In this instance, Pae, Dean, and Matt expressed a willingness to make amends, so plans for the hui did proceed.

The selection of the venue and time for the Hui Whakatika are determining factors. The principal's office is not a recommended venue, and any time between 9 am and 3 pm is not a suitable time. Not only is the principal's office likely to be too small; it may also trigger some uncomfortable memories for the student. Holding the hui during the school day is unsuitable; it is likely to rule out staff and whānau attending because of their day-to-day responsibilities, and it would place time constraints on people who are required to remain for the course of a hui that may go for, on average, 90 minutes.

It was decided, therefore, that the venue for this Hui Whakatika was to be a classroom at the school. The facilitators asked for a room with a large whiteboard (on which the story and plan could be mapped out) and for chairs to be arranged in a horseshoe so that people would be facing each other. The meeting was set for 6 pm.

There was one other important task to carry out before the hui. The DP was to call on a Māori elder, a kaumātua, and invite him to the meeting. Māori society generally values and respects ageing and older people. These people maintain positive roles and are afforded status not only because of their age, but also because of the very considerable skill and knowledge they bring. Kaumātua tend to live active lives, physically, socially, and culturally (Durie, Allan, Cunningham, Edwards, Gillies, Kingi, Ratima, & Waldon, 1997). They have a reverence, or wehi, which can often elicit respect from even the most challenging characters in our communities.

In due course, the Hui Whakatika was convened and 18 people attended (see Figure 7.3 below).

Figure 7.3 Participants in the Hui Whakatika for Pae, Dean, and Matt

Present at Hui Whakatika	
Pae, Dean, and Matt	Students
John	Kaumātua
Anthony	Deputy principal
Yvonne	Community education officer
Kelvin	Matt's father
Ana	Matt's mother
George	Pae's father
Dana	Pae's mother
Stephanie	Dean's mother
Logan	PE teacher, rugby coach of the three boys
Katrina	Pae's tutor, who had great faith in Pae
Bill	Teacher, who taught all three in the GAIN programme
Elizabeth	Kaitiaki and maths teacher
Kathie	Kaiawhina (teacher aide)
Moira	Kaitiaki (advisers), taught Pae and Matt
Ron	Technical arts teacher

The hui followed a sequence of prescribed steps, outlined in Figure 7.4 below.

The kaumātua commenced the hui with a karakia and a mihimihi (welcome) to the visitors and all those present. Staff from the school supported his kōrero

Figure 7.4 Prescribed sequence of steps for Hui Whakatika

Karakia/Welcome Response to welcome by manuhiri Introductions—Whakawhanungatanga
Tea and kai
How we are affected (aggression) Success so far (success) Barriers to continued success (enemies) The way forward (responsibilities) Karakia
Tea and kai
Informal discussion

(opening address) with a waiata (song), an indication that they too had prepared culturally, as well as socially, for the meeting. One of the facilitators responded in te reo Māori, and he and his colleague also supported the kōrero with a waiata. Here, representatives from both Treaty partners were demonstrating their keenness to work in te miro whero (the red strand). These practices of karakia, mihimihi, and waiata ensured that personal and spiritual connections were made. These key concepts instil warmth in and give integrity to the hui process. If the boys' deeds were deemed to be a violation of people's rights, then that needed to be addressed through tika, pono, and aroha—essential tonics in the healing, caring process. Tika refers to justice, pono to integrity, and aroha to compassion. Students like Pae, Dean, and Matt may not appear to manifest these qualities in abundance. They are qualities which may indeed have been suppressed or dominated by unhappy experiences, trauma, or failure. Therefore, they all need to be nurtured and have such qualities modelled by the adults around them.

The protocol of the Hui Whakatika requires that two processes need to precede the phase that addresses the kaupapa proper: introductions (whaka whanaungatanga) and refreshments (kai). Through whakawhanaungatanga, each person in the room, usually in order of seating, introduces themselves and says what their hopes and aspirations are for the meeting. The food is much more than merely sustenance for participants' physical wellbeing; it is the metaphor that signals hospitality and nourishment to the manuhiri (visitors), as well as kindness and care toward all concerned—manaakitanga. It also speaks of a sense of oneness, sharing, and unity—kōtahitanga.

When the Hui Whakatika reconvened (after the partaking of food), the facilitators asked people to tell the story of what had been happening and to name the problem. In this case it was named as "aggression". The concerns that had been documented about the boys' behaviour were recited from the facilitators' memory banks rather than from pages of written material. As others joined in with their contributions, it was then possible to map the effects of the problem. At all times, the kawa (protocol) of respecting individuals' contributions was upheld through the concept that "the one holding the rākau speaks", and speaks uninterrupted.

It was tactical and right to declare that the problem was the problem, the person was not the problem, despite the fact that it is often hard not to immediately want to apportion blame. A brief brainstorming exercise soon netted a variety of feelings with regard to the effect the problem was having on

Figure 7.5 Eliciting the effects of the problem

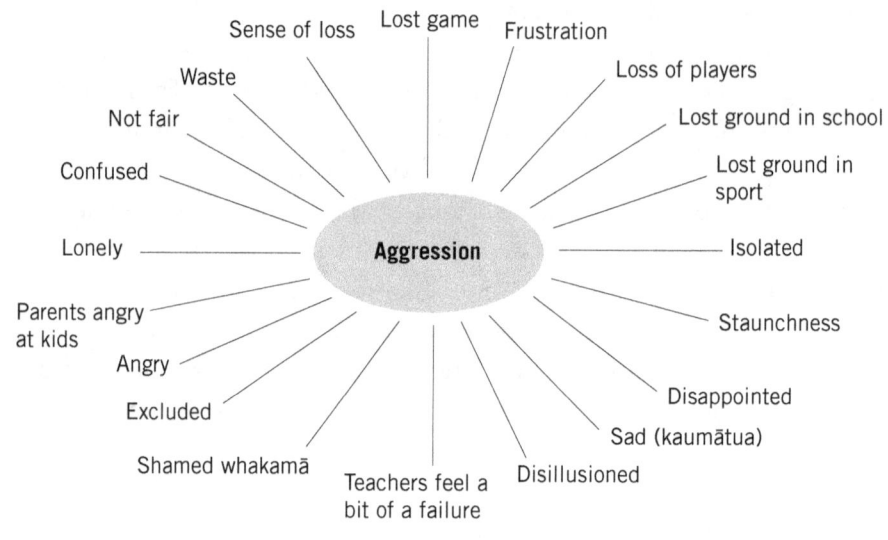

various people in the room. The whiteboard began to take on the appearance of spokes coming out from the hub of a wheel (see Figure 7.5).

While it is important to emphasise the effects of the problem, the discussions must not dwell there. These must move over to the successes that the students are experiencing at school, in class, and on the sports fields. Often, people are pleasantly surprised at the range of abilities that students in trouble actually possess and demonstrate. This exercise is usually extremely reinforcing and affirming for students, teachers, and parents, as was the case in the hui for Pae, Dean, and Matt.

The Hui Whakatika then moved on to the next phases, which identify the "enemies" to the boys succeeding in school (what is getting in their road?), seeking out new shoots, and formulating a plan for the road ahead. Pae, Dean, and Matt received many, and unexpected, positive affirmations throughout the discussions (such as how good they were at things, how much they were valued by others, what the problem was doing to others as well as themselves). When asked if they would like aggression to continue, or if they would like it to stop, they opted unanimously for the latter.

The Hui Whakatika determines that the planning ahead needs to be specific, related to the problem, committed to making amends, be feasible, indicate who will do what and where responsibilities will be shared, have clear timelines, and that the decisions made will be shared with others who should know. For Pae, Dean, and Matt, this meant that the current contract that was in place would be renegotiated. Some of the distal or far-off rewards for the students, when earned, would be made more proximal or close. This new contract would also include input from and responsibilities for the boys, the parents, and some teachers. One teacher, Logan, was to be the contact person for staff at the school. The kaumātua offered to take the boys through some tikanga classes. Another teacher offered to be the contact person for the parents. This would eliminate any fuss and embarrassment, obstacles that they had encountered in previous weeks. Another teacher offered her strengths and knowledge about drug awareness and anger management, and the parents agreed to set up a small support network amongst themselves. One interesting revelation, amongst many others, was that the parents had rarely been to watch their talented rugby-playing sons at a weekend fixture. Some of the parents made a pledge to do so, and the coach, Logan, was visibly delighted. So too were Pae, Dean, and Matt. A date for a review of the Hui Whakatika was made, and it was then time for closure.

The facilitators summed up by reiterating the main points that had emerged and the ideas that were developed in the discussions. They allayed any disconcerting notions, and reaffirmed the wholesomeness of the kaupapa (process). They signalled the new directions, and expressed the need for shared responsibility to continue as the helping (awhinatia) process moved on. The DP thanked everyone for attending and handed back to the kaumātua to officially close the Hui Whakatika with a mihi whakamutanga and karakia. Once again, food was shared before going home.

According to Drewery, Hooper, Macfarlane, McManemin, Pare, and Winslade (1998), the process of school, family and community group conferencing (SFCG) is *not* about stipulating who is to be in the room or what checklists should be attended to. It is about preparing to speak with each other about difficult things in a way that avoids regressing into the dynamics that gave rise to the problems in the first place.

In daily life, it is commonplace to encounter the use of punitive and judgemental forms of speech, particularly where there is a desire to "pull someone into line". These habits of judgement are hard to break. In this sense, conferencing is about developing new ways of speaking. All instances of conferencing are, by definition, intended to promote discussion. Speaking respectfully does not cost a great deal, and it can be extremely effective in achieving desirable outcomes. However, according to Drewery (2004), it is not always as straightforward as it sounds. Drewery and her colleagues from the University of Waikato (Cavanagh, 2005; Drewery et al., 1998; Hooper, Winslade, Drewery, Monk, & Macfarlane, 1999) are particularly interested in the types of conversations that are able to turn people and events around, not frighteningly, but firmly and fairly. The outcomes sought are to restore persons from a state of disorientation to a state of proportionality. The conversations are constantly searching for ways of going forward, searching for and developing new directions. The Hui Whakatika is a restorative practice that is underpinned by the Hikairo element awhinatia, helping individuals and groups who are on the margins and in need of a lifeline.

The hui, while bearing some resemblance to a family group conference (FGC), is also distinctive, because aspects of Māoritanga are given authentic appreciation and prominence. No long-term suspension or expulsion should be at all possible without first holding such a hui. The hui would need to involve the student and the significant people from his or her educational and community contexts. It would need to include any person who had been particularly affected by the problem. The group at the hui would be required to consider all the relevant matters, and then draw up a plan to address the concerns. McElrea (1997) contends that a good plan would obviously need to include aspects that would be of benefit to the school (e.g., nonviolence pacts, attendance undertakings), as well as aspects for the student's benefit (e.g., joining a sports club, receiving counselling). It may also need to include aspects for the benefit of the community (e.g., removal of graffiti), and that would be of benefit to the whānau (e.g., parent(s) to take an active interest in the school community).

The hui is a protocol-laden and structured process. It opens and closes in a certain fashion; there is an order as to who should speak and when. There is a place for talk and debate, laughter and tears, food and song. There is also a wairua, a spirituality, which exudes mana—and (as previously mentioned) mana can move people! The voices of te reo Māori, the whaikōrero of the kaumātua, the presence of whanaungatanga, and the intensity of the *take* (argument) are the *taonga tuku iho,* the treasures of history and mythology. Through the language, the culture, and the whānau, the history and traditional stories of Māori are able to be lived and experienced through the hui, which has traditionally been the focal point of Māori life—and for many, it still is. The hui comes in many forms. King (1993) points to the notions of:

Māori coming together to meet in these ways: to surpass the hospitality of previous hosts; to issue oratorical challenges and display astonishing feats of memory in the recitation of genealogy and tradition; to debate; to display prowess in haka, action song, taiaha, and canoe handling. (p. 77)

There is thus a strong argument that the hui is a most appropriate process to provide support and help to Māori students with behaviour difficulties, and their whānau.

The hui is an art, in that while it subscribes to prescriptions and routines, it is also influenced by qualities and contingencies that are unpredictable. All those present at the hui find themselves being drawn into a "whānau of interest" (Bishop & Glynn, 1998), and the ends that are achieved are often created in the process. There is an analogy here with Eisner's (1994) "four senses of the art of teaching", where he proposes that the experience of teaching can be aesthetic, heuristic, adventitious, and emergent. The genuine hui adopts all of those qualities. Maybe educators need to question the appropriateness of the sometimes mechanical approaches that are often adopted, such as the FGC. Such contexts, it is argued, when bereft of hui qualities, may only serve to minimise opportunities, outcomes, and successes relating to restorative processes.

In New Zealand, to a large extent, the curricula, teaching methodologies, and teacher training associated with schooling are based on a world view that does not always recognise or acknowledge the importance of Māori concepts and values and the central place of whānau in Māori society. The Hui Whakatika is one humble approach that is able to support students with behaviour difficulties, and their whānau. This approach acknowledges the importance of Māori concepts and ecologies. Helpers of youngsters in trouble—classroom teachers, deans, counsellors, RTLB, and GSE personnel—are at the interface of developing a helping system that respects the philosophical and pedagogical foundations provided by both Māori and non-Māori cultural traditions. That is the challenge. Me haere whakamua tātou: let us value inclusion as we move forward, educulturally, together (Macfarlane, cited in Fraser et al., 2005).

Tōia te waka mātauranga
Mā wai e tō? Māku e tō, māu e tō
Mā te whakaranga ake e tō
Haul forth the canoe of education
Who should haul it? I should, you should
All within calling distance should haul the canoe

Orangatanga: developing a nurturing environment

Te Rākau (Figure 7.2) depicts the element of orangatanga as the roots of the tree. Tree roots anchor the tree in the soil, keeping it straight and stable. Tree roots absorb water from the soil, take nutrients out of the soil, and use them to produce what they need for the tree's growth and development (Angus & Gay, 1992). Just as the root system of a tree performs many vital functions, so too does the teacher in establishing and maintaining a healthy and well nourished classroom climate.

The Hikairo Rationale has described a range of approaches and techniques for preventing and responding to behaviour difficulties in the classroom. The Rationale also offers procedures for establishing rules and supporting students to comply with them. It provides exercises to help teachers gain insight into the importance of demeanour, attitude, patience, and dignity.

The dignity of the student and the dignity of the teacher are the roots of a nurturing learning environment. Lucas (cited in Senge et al., 2000) reasons that teachers may regularly talk about curriculum content, teaching methods, and, occasionally, new research or multiple ways of learning. But how often are their conversations about valuing and respecting each child? How often do conversations consider how teachers perceive the young people in their care through a lens of dignity?

The elements of the Hikairo Rationale have, in various ways, provided strategies about setting a context that will promote and foster a productive and enjoyable learning environment. In many instances, the rationale calls for teachers to encourage interactive learning, to get to know their students, to be assertive, to have a positive attitude, and to exude a passion for their work. Students of all ages observe and recognise these qualities in their teachers, and they like them. They see these teachers as role models, and draw from the behavioural positives. As well as in-school factors, the rationale offers strategies for out-of-school factors, such as the Hui Whakatika.

The elements of the Hikairo Rationale are, collectively, about attaining a sense of place within the general scheme of things; they are about belonging. Ryan and Stiller (1991) contend that when students experience a sense of belonging in a school context, they are more likely to relate to the goals and values of the school. In contrast, a context that does not allow students to experience a sense of belonging will diminish motivation, and may ultimately lead to alienation and poor performance. Wehlage, Rutter, Smith, Lesko, and

Fernandez (cited in Alderman, 1999) identify four social bonds that connect students to the school:

> *Attachment:* Students are socially bonded to the extent that they have social and emotional ties to adults and peers in the school. This attachment is reciprocal: 'The school/teacher cares about me and I care about my actions.' Therefore, students have a vested interest in meeting expectations of others and abiding by the norms of behaviour expected in the school.
>
> *Commitment:* Social bonds are formed by commitment, a conscious decision by students about what they have to do to contribute to their own and the school's goals (e.g. working in classes where they have no real interest). If students do not have hope for the future, commitment is less likely. This social bond is critical and brings into play the role of accountability and the artistry of the teacher.
>
> *Involvement:* Student involvement in school activities, both academic and non-academic, increases the likelihood of bonding. If students are not active participants in school, they are more often disengaged, as evidenced by their passivity.
>
> *Belief:* Students' belief that an education is important, and their faith in the school to provide them with an education, is asserted by Newmann (1992) to be the bedrock of membership. The first three factors (attachment, commitment and involvement) are somewhat dependent on this one. This is also about a reciprocal relationship, requiring that teachers also believe that students are competent to learn and achieve their own goals. (p. 173)

It is important to try to relate the concepts of these four social bonds to concepts that are meaningful within a Māori world view. Orangatanga is a state that becomes possible where the mauri (life force) of the student is vibrant, where hā (essence) breathes freely, allowing for the manifestation of confidence and the enhancement of performance.

The Hikairo Rationale: drawing it all together

Western European metaphors and illustrations are not uncommon in explanations of holistic approaches to human development, health, and education. For example, the micro, meso, and macrosystems influencing human development as identified by Bronfenbrenner (1979). Similarly, Māori representations are also offered to describe a Māori holistic view of the world. Such a view is often conceptualised as the state where body, mind, and spirit are not separate entities, but are interlinked to capture the concept of "wholeness".

Irwin (1984, p. 6) illustrates the concept of wholeness and loss of wholeness by the full and incomplete triangles where each side represents one of the dimensions of body, mind, and spirit. While Irwin's depiction of an holistic world view is an effective one, his model is taken a step further by Durie (1994), who extends the triangle to a four-sided figure in order to incorporate a fourth dimension, that of whānau, within the construction of individual identity and wellbeing. This model, Te Whare Tapa Whā, is represented as the four walls of a house with each side complementing the others.

In a similar way, Pere's Te Wheke (1991) expresses an holistic health and education model for sustaining self through the metaphor of the octopus. Four tentacles embrace the cornerstones inherent in Te Whare Tapa Whā, but the other four give substance to the importance of mana ake (status), mauri (life force), hā a koro mā a kui mā (breath of life coming from the tipuna), and whatumanawa (emotional life). Waiora, or complete wellbeing, is said to be found when each tentacle, or dimension of wellbeing, receives sufficient sustenance. Te Wheke acknowledges the link between the mind, spirit, and whānau with the physical world in a way that is seamless.

The Hikairo Rationale acknowledges the depth and insightfulness that Te Whare Tapa Whā and Te Wheke offer professionals in the fields of health and education. In a very humble way, the Hikairo Rationale also includes the elements of te rākau to the field of behaviour methodology. When the strategies and techniques inherent in the Hikairo elements are effectively applied, students experiencing behaviour difficulties may indeed have a greater chance of reaching their full potential and experience opportunities to take their place more meaningfully in their classrooms, schools, whānau, and community. At the root of providing sustenance for young people reaching toward more abounding prospects is orangatanga, a nurturing environment.

The four walls of Te Whare Tapa Whā (Durie, 1994), the eight tentacles and the eye of Te Wheke (Pere, 1991), and the elements of the Hikairo Rationale as depicted in Te Rākau all fit together and are connected. Each needs to be interpreted in relation to the other aspects of the sociocultural orientation that they represent. They are not just a collection of variables that operate independently. They co-exist in a similar fashion to Rogoff's (2003) description of the way social practices fit together: "They vary together in patterned ways" (p. 11). A reductionist approach to explaining the variables would fail to recognise the coherence among the constellations of features that make up the whole.

In making meaning of the sociocultural understandings of the Hikairo Rationale, the value of some Western theories was taken into consideration. This allowed for a synthesis of global knowledge and indigenous wisdom (what Macfarlane (2006) refers to as "educultural") to be posited. Take, for instance, the compatibility of the Hikairo Rationale with Glasser's (1975) considerations on human progress. Glasser is in tandem with the concept of mana, wherein a person gains strength by progressing along four success pathways: giving and receiving love; achieving a sense of worth in one's own eyes and in the eyes of others; having fun; and becoming self-disciplined.

The Hikairo Rationale encourages teachers to take a step back and reflect on the meaning of the mana of the individual. The rationale focuses on learning and teaching strategies that promote respect and dignity. Without exception, each strategy of the Hikairo Rationale hinges on sound and caring relationships, so that a quality learning and teaching environment can exist.

The roots, arteries, and branches of Te Rākau represent a collection of methods and strategies for educators; they are offered to help educators in their work with students who are experiencing learning and behaviour difficulties. There are no guarantees in the realm of learning and behaviour, but as change agents educators must believe that they *can* make a difference. The Hikairo Rationale proposes that, like a tree, educators must be prepared for each season, and be there to provide shelter for those who need it.

> *Ki te kore te pūtake e mākūkūngia*
> *E kore te rākau e tupu*
> If the roots of the tree are not watered
> The tree will never grow

PART FOUR

SYNTHESIS

Unity of purpose as a basis for action

8 Navigating the choppy sea

CHAPTER 8

Navigating the choppy sea

Introduction

In every profession, there comes a time when it is important to pause and evaluate the progress that has been made, and to determine the changes that will be necessary to engage with new times and meet new demands. The professional practice of teaching is no exception (Macfarlane, 2007). In a time of rapid change, many solutions are offered about what it takes to sustain effort in order to achieve success. Some of these solutions for the acquisition of quality in education insist on precision, rigour, and consistency in teachers' approaches to classroom practice, and replicability of classroom programmes. Many teachers are skilled in achieving solutions through all, if not most, of those means; others struggle to achieve some, if any, of the solutions. This is often put down to the increasingly demanding workload of teachers:

> There is little doubt that the workload of teachers (much like other professions) has increased and to some degree changed in scope over recent decades. Teachers face ever increasing reporting and compliance requirements resulting in an increase in paperwork and administration. There has been an inordinate pace of change in curriculum and assessment which is perceived to have been poorly supported and too rapidly imposed. Increasingly teachers have been called upon to address social issues that arise in society for which they are ill-prepared and which draw

attention away from a focus on supporting learning. The behaviour of children and young people has become more challenging and teachers face increasing expectations from parents and the Ministry to meet the individual needs of all students. The increasing workload has drawn attention to the need for teachers to prioritise work-life balance to ensure they can do their jobs effectively. (Ministry of Education, 2006b, p. 6)

Teachers are key figures in the lives of children and young people going to school. While attending to the mandated curriculum, teachers also provide significant social and emotional security for many students, who may be disaffected due to a wide range of variables in their lives. But teachers provide this care at a cost. In a study of job satisfaction and teacher stress in New Zealand primary schools, teachers rated disruptive students, inadequate remuneration, and task overload as sources of moderate stress. They rated lack of respect for teachers and teaching as sources of mild to moderate stress. The actual numbers of students with serious learning and behaviour difficulties in a class affected job stress and job satisfaction (Prochnow et al., 2000). What can we do to help teachers who are in these situations?

More questions than answers?

Responding to that question raises even more questions about what it means for schools, in terms of understanding their reality when it comes down to dealing with students with behaviour difficulties. The most striking feature of the behaviour conundrum is the sheer variety of causes, and responses to, behaviour difficulties that are manifested in schools. This is a complex issue that does not lend itself to simple solutions. Any quest for one dominant remedy would be futile.

However, while completely eliminating behaviour difficulties in schools is not possible, reducing them is a realistic aim. A starting point would be to consider three basic questions. Senge and his colleagues suggest that schools look within their own organisation in their quest to know more about where they are positioned, and how they wish to make progress in terms of a particular issue. The questions that they could usefully ask are:
- Does our school have a clear and honest understanding of its current reality?
- Is the understanding of the current reality shared throughout the school?
- Is knowledge translated into effective action toward our desired future?

(Senge et al., 2000, pp. 552–553)

These questions are posed so as to generate healthy discussion that will challenge underlying assumptions, explore capabilities, and search for priorities that might provide direction along a desired pathway. Perhaps this inward searching and reflection will lead to the school developing a unified purpose that will serve as a springboard for action.

A whole-school behaviour-management programme

One such development might be revisiting or creating a whole-school behaviour management programme. The development of such a programme is an immensely important task, given that behaviour difficulties are not confined to the classroom alone; they exist and need to be managed across all contexts within a school. Bennett (cited in Wheldall, 1992) considers that the policies which inform a whole-school behaviour-management programme need to support, promote, and encourage good behaviour, and should also provide opportunities for teaching and rewarding it. He tempers this with a reality check, stating that it is also necessary to clearly outline the expectations as well as the boundaries, including distinct consequences should breeches occur. In addition, shared ownership of the policy and programme is crucial:

> If a whole-school behaviour policy is to succeed it will need to be tailor-made to the precise requirements of the individual school. That is why it can only be devised by those who have inside knowledge of the school's life and work. It will also need to be rational and intelligible to all the people involved and the whole-school community will need to give willing support to its precepts and try to live by them. That end is not likely to be achieved if the policy is seen as something imposed from on high. The policy needs to evolve through a process of wide consultation with teachers, ancillary staff, pupils, parents and governors all feeling that their views have been heard, fairly considered and incorporated. In that way the whole-school behaviour policy ought to secure a wide measure of support. (Bennett, 1992, p. 7)

Richmond School

It appears that Doig (2000) heeded these wise words. While on a Beeby Fellowship with the New Zealand Council for Educational Research, Doig reported on how Richmond School had developed a successful whole-school behaviour-management programme. Echoing Bennett's advice that whole-school behaviour-management programmes must not be premised on a "one size fits all" model, Doig claims that unless all staff members own and drive their own programme, based on their own particular issues, needs, and resources, then it is largely a waste of time.

For Richmond School, starting with a set of beliefs was seen as critical, and from that position a number of key elements in school behaviour were identified. The key elements included the building of positive relationships, developing and maintaining good classroom tone, and creating a positive playground climate where safety and peace prevailed. The staff of Richmond School were adamant that clear systems, policies, and procedures definitely helped their school to focus on prevention, rather than cure. The prevention of problem behaviour also reduced teacher stress levels—another powerful reason to invest time and energy into collaboratively developing a whole-school approach to managing behaviour.

Navigating the choppy sea

A notable Māori whakatauki (proverb) states: "He moana pukepuke e ekengia—a choppy sea can be navigated." Achieving consensus about and consistency across a school-wide behaviour-management programme is not an easy task for school administrators and classroom teachers. Given the many and complex mandatory requirements placed upon schools (teacher appraisal, ERO visits, curriculum reviews and updates, assessment, and reporting), staff may well feel that the task of developing and implementing a whole-school behaviour-management programme is not a top priority. This stresses the importance of remaining resolute and persevering.

Figure 8.1 aims to provide a helpful compass for navigating the choppy sea. This pragmatic framework sets out a number of guiding principles. It outlines the levels of challenging behaviour and the corresponding level of resourcing and support, as well as the system (or approach) that would be the most applicable at certain points within the framework. In the final analysis, individual schools need to develop their own behaviour policies and programmes, tailored to their particular context and culture.

An effective whole-school behaviour-management programme will come into being only if all those who have a role to play within it know what to do to make it effective, and how to do this well. Senior administrators and lead teachers will have to organise and manage the programme successfully, as well as "branding" it to parents in a way that gives the community faith that the school can make a difference to those inside it, and to the community outside it. Behaviour programmes and policies are more likely to succeed if the culture

Figure 8.1 The behaviour compass (Macfarlane, 2007)

GUIDING PRINCIPLES
- An inclusive and safe environment is critical
- Intent on promoting trends of behaviour that enhance an orderly learning community
- Intent on addressing behaviour issues that are causing concern
- Staff have a common understanding and a consistent response repertoire of behaviour and motivation strategies
- Good teaching matters

He moana pukepuke e ekengia e te waka
A choppy sea can be navigated
"Persevere: never give up"

LEVEL ONE
- Behaviours are mild to moderate
- Problems are environmentally and systems related
- Intervention based on prevention
- Option of RTLB involvement
- Good teaching matters

- Low end need
- Low resourcing required per student or programme

System: Straightforward intervention strategies dominate

DEMOCRACY

LEVEL TWO
- Behaviours are moderate to severe
- Problems caused by an interaction between environmental and personal factors
- Intervention based on prevention and redirection
- Option of GSE involvement
- Good teaching matters

- Moderate need
- Medium resourcing required per student or programme

System: A comprehensive and integrated programmatic approach may be required

DISCIPLINE

LEVEL THREE
- Behaviours are severe to serious
- Problems tend to be more often caused by environmental and psychological factors
- Intervention based on prevention, redirection and suppression
- Option of outside agency involvement
- Good teaching matters

- High need
- High resourcing required per student or programme

System: Special education for emotional and health considerations may be required

DIVERSITY

System: Care and perseverance

of the school is a healthy one. An effective culture and ethos, while difficult to define, is one that keeps sending out a message that this is a positive, hard-working place—a successful school.

Successful schools do not just happen. According to Roger Smith (2002), they do not just come into existence by waving a magic wand. They require hard work and systematic planning. Arguably, becoming a successful school is incumbent on good teaching:

> In other words, everyone has to do their job well because no one who works in schools wants to be thought of as ineffective and no teacher, head teacher, trustee, parent or child wants their school to be seen as under-performing and unsuccessful. One excellent teacher in a mediocre school will not make the school effective but one bad teacher in an otherwise successful school will bring down its level of effectiveness significantly. Everyone will have to work together to achieve high standards. (pp. 1–2)

Smith's (2002) notions on effective and ineffective teachers are compatible with Hattie's (2003) assertion that it is the teachers that are the greatest point of difference, and that attention needs to be directed at higher quality teaching. Add to that Wylie's (2006) simple but profound claim that the actions of teachers are uppermost in terms of making a difference in young people's lives, and the prognosis that "the teacher calls the tune" becomes an almost irrefutable one.

However, teachers are people too. The physiological and psychological effects of dealing with the many facets of teaching can lead to negative feelings about self and work, fatigue, moodiness, and lack of motivation. Such feelings are not unusual in any job. But because teaching is a special vocation that involves people on an expansive scale, it is essential that teachers have some ways of coping with these feelings. According to Gersch (1996), some effective strategies include: constructing lists of things to do; prioritising; having a mentor to talk to; and having leisure activities and hobbies. Teachers are not a stand-alone entity—they are a key part of a natural alliance between themselves, parents, students, and school administration on the issue of self-respect and respect for others. This alliance must be underpinned by the values and beliefs they have identified on a collective basis, i.e., as a staff. Bransgrove and Jesson (1993) and Macfarlane, Glynn, Cavanagh, and Bateman (2006) contend that, reduced to their most fundamental characteristics, the factors that contribute to effective learning and teaching are:

- sound relationships between teachers and students
- democratic practices in the classroom

- realistic expectations of the learner
- relevance of the learning experiences to the students' culture, interests, and their prior experiences
- humanity from the teacher.

In classrooms where these factors are adopted, more meaningful learning takes place. In such classrooms, teachers usually: adopt a position that regards students as autonomous and responsible learners; provide students with opportunities for doing things differently—within reason; conduct authentic assessments that directly guide teaching; and work patiently and skilfully with students experiencing behaviour difficulties.

Working with students with behaviour difficulties can be frustrating for many teachers. However, when teachers are provided with proactive strategies for promoting young people's social and academic development, working with these students can be transformed into a rewarding challenge. When strategies, such as those outlined in earlier chapters, are implemented consistently and with a high degree of integrity, the need for individualised intervention steadily decreases. However, despite teachers' best efforts, some students will continue to present challenges. That is not an excuse to desist. The philosophy of inclusion requires teachers to invest considerable efforts in coping when these challenges arise.

The importance of employing skilled and practical processes for responding to students with behaviour difficulties underscores the need to reconsider the type of preparation offered by faculties of education as they prepare people to enter the profession of teaching. Practising teachers also require regular and ongoing professional development because of the need to increase their awareness of progressive educational research activities so as to replete their knowledge and skills with regard to proactive approaches to working with students with behaviour difficulties. Preservice training and inservice professional development must be geared toward advancing the acquisition of knowledge, skills, and strategies that will help teachers to crystallise a balanced approach to discipline—one that fosters democracy and values diversity.

References

A $4.5m fund to manage unruly kids. (2007, 21 February). *The Dominion Post*, p. A10.

Alberti, R., & Emmons, M. (1986). *Your perfect right: A guide to assertive living.* San Luis Obispo, CA: Impact Publishers.

Alderman, M. K. (1999). *Motivation and achievement: Possibilities for teaching and learning.* Mahwah, NJ: Lawrence Erlbaum Associates.

Andrews, J., & Lupart, J. (1993). *The inclusive classroom: Educating exceptional learners.* Scarborough, Ontario: International Thomson Publishing.

Angus, K., & Gay, P. (1992). *Trees in our world.* Wellington: Learning Media in association with Ministry of Forestry.

Arthur, M., Gordon, C., & Butterfield, N. (2003). *Classroom management: Creating positive learning environments.* Southbank, Vicoria: Thomson.

Ashman, A., & Elkins, J. (Eds.). (1998). *Educating children with special needs* (3rd ed.). Sydney: Prentice-Hall.

Ashman, A., & Elkins, J. (Eds.). (2002). *Educating children with diverse abilities.* Sydney: Prentice-Hall.

Axelson, J. (Ed.). (1993). *Counseling and development in a multicultural society* (2nd ed.). Pacific Grove, CA: Brooks/Cole Publishing.

Balson, M. (1992). *Understanding classroom behaviour.* Hawthorn, Victoria: Australian Council for Educational Research.

Bandura, A. (1977). *Social learning theory.* Englewood Cliffs, NJ: Prentice Hall.

Barlow, C. (1993). *Tikanga whakaaro: Key concepts in Māori culture.* Auckland: Oxford University Press.

Bateman, S. (2003). *Te kupenga o te manaaki: The net of replenishment: A collaborative process for data gathering and assessment.* Presentation given at the University of Waikato, Hamilton, 2005.

Bateman, S. (2007). *Culturally inclusive classrooms: Making it work for you, and for them.* Presentation to preservice teachers, University of Waikato, Hamilton, 5 September.

Bennett, R. (1992). Discipline in schools: The Report of the Committee of Enquiry chaired by Lord Elton. In K. Wheldall, *Discipline in schools: Psychological perspectives on the Elton Report* (pp.1–9). London: Routledge.

Bevan-Brown, J. (2005). A snap-shot of organisational provisions for Māori children and youth with special needs. *Kairaranga Journal of Educational Practice, 6(1),* 3–10.

Bevan-Brown, J. (2006). Beyond policy and good intentions. *International Journal of Inclusive Education, 10(2–3),* 221–234.

Beveridge, S. (1995). *Special education needs in schools.* London: Routledge.

Bishop, R. (1996a). Addressing issues of self-determination and legitimation in kaupapa Māori research. In B. Webber (Ed.), *He Paepae Kōrero: Research perspectives in Māori education* (pp. 143–160). Wellington: New Zealand Council for Educational Research.

Bishop, R. (1996b). *Collaborative research stories: Whakawhanaungatanga.* Palmerston North: Dunmore Press.

Bishop, R., & Berryman, M. (2006). *Culture speaks: Cultural relationships and classroom learning.* Wellington: Huia Publishers.

Bishop, R., Berryman, M., Tiakiwai, S., & Richardson, C. (2002). *Te Kōtahitanga: The experiences of year 9 and year 10 Māori students in mainstream classrooms.* A research report to the Ministry of Education. Hamilton: University of Waikato.

Bishop, R., Berryman, M., Tiakiwai, S., & Richardson, C. (2003). *Te Kōtahitanga: The experiences of year 9 and 10 Māori students in mainstream classrooms.* A final report to the Ministry of Education. Hamilton: University of Waikato. Retrieved from (undated), http://www.minedu.govt.nz/goto/tekotahitanga

Bishop, R., & Glynn, T. (1998). Achieving cultural integrity within education in New Zealand. In K. Cushner (Ed.), *Intercultural perspectives on intercultural education* (pp. 38–70). New York: Lawrence Erlbaum Associates.

Bishop, R., & Glynn, T. (1999). *Culture counts: Changing power relations in education.* Palmerston North: Dunmore Press.

Blumberg, A. (1989). *School administration as a craft: Foundations of practice.* Boston: Allyn & Bacon.

Bos, C., & Vaughn, S. (1998). *Strategies for teaching students with learning and behavior problems* (4th ed.). Boston: Allyn & Bacon.

Bower, E. (1981). *Early identification of emotionally hanidcapped children in school* (3rd ed.). Springfield, IL: Charles C. Thomas.

Bransgrove, E., & Jesson, A. (1993). A matter of survival: Stress and the emergency teacher. *set: Research Information for Teachers, 1* (item 6), 1–4.

Brigham, F., & Brigham, M. (2005). *An introduction to understanding behavior.* Virginia, VA: University of Virginia.

Brigham, F. J., & Cole, J. E. (1998). Selective mutism: Developments in definition, etiology, assessment and treatment. In T. E. Scruggs & M. A. Mastropieri (Eds.), *Advances in learning and behavioral disabilities* (pp. 183–216). Greenwich, CT: JAI Press.

Bronfenbrenner, U. (1979). *The ecology of human development: Experiments by nature and design.* Cambridge, MA: Harvard University Press.

Brown, D., & Thomson, C. (2000). *Cooperative learning in New Zealand schools.* Palmerston North: Dunmore Press.

Brown, D., Thomson, C., Anderson, A., Moore, D., Walker, J., Glynn, T., Macfarlane, A., Medcalf, J., & Ysseldyke, J. (2000). Resource teachers learning and behaviour: An ecological approach to special education. *Australasian Journal of Special Education, 24*(1), 5–20.

Bruner, J. (1996). *The culture of education.* London: Harvard University Press.

Burgess, B. (1992). *Referring at-risk students to activity centres.* MEd thesis. Palmerston North: Massey University.

Canter, L., & Canter, M. (1992). *Assertive discipline: Positive behavior management for today's classroom.* Santa Monica, CA: Lee Canter & Associates.

Casey, K. (1993). *I answer with my life.* New York: Routledge & Kegan Paul.

Cavanagh, T. (2003, August). Schooling for peace: Caring for our children in school. *Experiments in Education, 31*(8), 139–143.

Cavanagh, T. (2005). *Restoration practices and a culture of care in schools: A story of alternative positive peace efforts.* Preliminary report to Raglan Area School, Raglan.

Charles, C. (1999). *Building classroom discipline* (6th ed.). New York: Addison Wesley Longman.

Charles, C. (2002). *Building classroom discipline* (7th ed.). New York: Addison Wesley Longman.

City head fails MP for poor homework on pass rates. (2006, 23 November). *Hamilton This Week,* p. 4.

Clark, E., Smith, L., & Pomare, M. (1996). *Alternative education provisions.* Discussion Paper. Wellington: Te Puni Kokiri.

Cole, P., & Chan, L. (1990). *Methods and strategies for special education.* Sydney: Prentice-Hall.

Conway, R. (1998). Meeting the needs of students with behavioural and emotional problems. In A. Ashman & J. Elkins (Eds.). *Educating children with special needs* (3rd. ed., (pp. 177–228). Sydney: Prentice Hall.

Conway, R. (1999). Adapting curriculum and management strategies to support students with special needs in the inclusive classroom. *set special, 6, pp.* 1–4.

Cook, B., Tankersley, M., Cook, L., & Landrum, T. (2000). Teachers' attitudes toward their included students with disabilities. *Exceptional Children, 67*(1), 115–135.

Cookson-Cox, C. (2006). *A perspective on truancy amongst young people in the Rotorua District.* Rotorua: Rotorua District Council.

Cooper, G., Arago-Kemp, V., Wylie, C., & Hodgen, E. (2004). *Te Rerenga ā te Pīrere: A longitudinal study of kōhanga reo and kura kaupapa Māori students: Phase one report.* Wellington: New Zealand Council for Educational Research.

Cross, T. L., Bazron, B. J., Dennis, K. W., & Isaacs, M. R. (1989). *Towards a culturally competent system of care* (Vol 1). Washington, DC: National Technical Assistance Centre for Children's Mental Health, Georgetown University Child Development Centre.

Davies, T., & Prangnell, A. (1999, September). *Special education 2000—A national framework.* Paper presented at the Australian Association of Special Education national conference, Sydney.

Doig, C. (2000). *Quality the Richmond way: Developing a successful behaviour managemet programme.* Wellington: New Zealand Council for Educational Research.

Doyle, W. (1986). Classroom organization and management. In M. C. Wittrock (Ed.), *Handbook of research on teaching* (3rd ed., pp. 392–431). New York: Macmillan.

Drewery, W. (2004). Conferencing in schools: Punishment, restorative justice, and the productive importance of the process of conversation. *Journal of Community and Applied Social Psychology, 14,* 332–344.

Drewery, W., Hooper, S., Macfarlane, A., McManemin, D., Pare, D., & Winslade, J. (1998). *School, family and community group conferencing.* Proposal to the Ministry of Education. Hamilton: University of Waikato.

Dunckley, I. (2005). *Managing extreme behaviour in schools.* Wellington: Ministry of Education.

Durie, M. (1994). *Whaiora: Māori health development.* Auckland: Oxford University Press.

Durie, M. (2003). *Ngā Kāhui pou: Launching Māori futures.* Wellington: Huia Publishers.

Durie, M., Allan, G., Cunningham, C., Edwards, W., Gillies, A., Kingi, T. R., Ratima, M., & Waldon, J. (1997). *Oranga kaumātua: The health and wellbeing of older Māori people.* Report prepared for the Ministry of Health and Te Puni Kōkiri. Palmerston North: Massey University.

Dyson, A., & Gains, C. (1993). *Rethinking special needs in mainstream schools: Towards the year 2000.* London: David Fulton Publishers.

Edmonds, R. (1979). Some schools work and more can. *Social Policy, 9*(5), 25–29.

Education and Science Committee of the House of Representatives. (1995). Inquiry into children in education at risk through truancy and behavioural problems. *Report of the Education and Science Committee, First Session, Forty Fourth Parliament.*

Educators told that violence on the rise in New Zealand Schools. (1995). *Education Weekly, 5*(200), 1.

Eisner, E. (1994). *The educational imagination: On the design and evaluation of school programs* (3rd ed.). New York: Macmillan.

Erikson, E. (1968). *Identity, youth, and crisis.* New York: W. W. Norton.

Felsenstein, D. (1987). *Comprehensive achievements.* Sevenoaks, UK: Hodder and Stoughton.

Fine, M. J. (Ed.). (1989). *The second handbook on parent education.* San Diego, CA: Academic.

Ford, B., Obiakor, F., & Patton, J. (Eds.). (1995). *Effective education of African-American exceptional learners: New perspectives.* Austin, TX: Pro-Ed.

Forlin, C. (1997, September). *The inclusive curriculum: What regular class teachers find stressful and how they cope.* Paper presented at the Australian Association of Special Education (AASE) 21st national conference, Brisbane, Australia.

Franklin, B. (Ed.). (1998). *When children don't learn: Student failure and the culture of teaching.* New York: Teachers College Press.

Fraser, D. (1995). Students with behavioural difficulties. In D. Fraser, R. Moltzen, & K. Ryba (Eds.), *Learners with special needs in Aotearoa/New Zealand* (pp. 229–266). Palmerston North: Dunmore Press.

Fraser, D, (2004). Secular schools, spirituality and Māori values. *Journal of Moral Education, 33*(1), 87–95.

Fraser, D., Moltzen, R., & Ryba, K. (1995). *Learners with special needs in Aotearoa/New Zealand.* Palmerston North: Dunmore Press.

Fraser, D., Moltzen, R., & Ryba, K. (2000). *Learners with special needs in Aotearoa/New Zealand* (2nd ed.). Palmerston North: Dunmore Press.

Fraser, D., Moltzen, R., & Ryba, K. (2005). *Learners with special needs in Aotearoa/New Zealand* (3rd ed.). Palmerston North: Dunmore Press.

Fuchs, D., & Fuchs, L. (1994). Inclusive schools movement and the radicalization of special education reform. *Exceptional Children, 60*(4), 294–309.

Fullan, M. G., & Hargreaves, A. (1991). *Working together for your school.* Hawthorn, Victoria: Australian Council for Educational Research.

Gadd, B. (1976). *Cultural difference in the classroom: Special needs of Māori in Pākehā schools.* Auckland: Heinemann Education.

Gay, G. (2000). *Culturally responsive teaching: Theory, research and practice.* New York: Teachers College Press.

Gersch, I. S. (1996). Teachers are people too. Support for learning: Special issue on children with emotional and/or behavioural difficulties. *British Journal of Learning Support, 11*(4), 165–169.

Glasser, W. (1975). *Reality therapy: A new approach to psychiatry.* New York: Harper & Row.

Glasser, W. (1992). *Quality school: Managing students without coercion.* New York: Harper Perennial.

Glynn, T., Berryman, M., Atvars, K., & Harawira, W. (1997). *Hei Awhina Maatua: A home and school behavioural programme.* Final report to the Ministry of Education. Wellington: Ministry of Education.

Glynn, T., Wearmouth, J., & Berryman, M. (2005). *Supporting students with literacy difficulties: A responsive approach.* London: McGraw-Hill Education.

Good, T., & Brophy, J. (1994). *Looking in classrooms.* New York: HarperCollins.

Goodlad, J. (1997). *In praise of education.* New York: Teachers College Press.

Graham, J. (2003). Kānohi ki te kānohi: Establishing partnerships between schools and Māori communities. In *set: Research Information for Teachers, 2,* 8–12.

Gray, J., & Richer, J. (1992). *Classroom responses to disruptive behaviour.* London: Routledge.

Grossman, H. (2004). *Classroom behavior management for diverse and inclusive schools* (3rd ed.). New York: Rowman & Littlefield.

Gudykunst, W. (1994). *Bridging differences: Effective intergroup communication.* Thousand Oaks, CA: Sage Publications.

Guevremont, D., & Dumas, M. (1994). Peer relationship problems and disruptive behavior disorders. *Journal of Emotional and Behavioral Disorders, 2,* 164–172.

Hallahan, D. P., & Kauffman, J. M. (1988). *Exceptional Children: Introduction to special education* (4th ed.), Englewood Cliffs, NJ: Prentice-Hall.

Hardman, M., Drew, C., & Egan, M. W. (1999). *Human exceptionality, society, school and family* (6th ed.). Sydney: Allyn & Bacon.

Hattie, J. (2003, February). *New Zealand education snapshot: With specific reference to the 1-13 years.* Presentation at Knowledge Wave 2003: The Leadership Forum. Auckland: University of Auckland.

Hill, J., & Hawk, K. (2000). *Making a difference in the classroom: Effective teaching practice in low decile, multicultural schools.* A report prepared for the Ministry of Education and AIMHI Forum. Albany: Institute for Professional Development and Educational Research, Massey University.

Hooper, S., Winslade, J., Drewery, W., Monk, G., & Macfarlane, A. (1999, July). *School and family group conferences: Te Hui Whakatika (a time for making amends).* Paper presented at the Keeping Young People in School Summit conference, Auckland.

Hoover, J. J., & Patton, J. R. (1997). *Curriculum adaptations for students with learning and behavior problems* (2nd ed.). Austin, TX: Pro-Ed.

Hopkins. (2004). *Just schools: A whole school approach to restorative justice.* London: Jessica Kinsley Publishers.

Irwin, J. (1984). *An introduction to Māori religion.* Bedford Park, South Australia: Australian Association for the Study of Religions.

Jenkins, G. (1961). *Helping children reach their potential.* Chicago: Scott Foresman.

Jensen, E. (1995). *Super teaching.* San Diego, CA: The Brain Store.

Johnson D., Johnson, R., & Maruyama, G. (1983). Interdependence and interpersonal attraction among heterogeneous and homogeneous individuals: A theoretical formulation and meta-analysis of the research. *Review of Educational Research, 52*(1), 5–54.

Jones, A. (1989). The cultural production of classroom practice. *British Journal of Sociology of Education, 10*(1), 19–31.

Jones, F. (1987). *Positive classroom discipline.* New York: McGraw-Hill.

Jones, V. F. (1992). Integrating behavioural and insight-oriented treatment on school-based programs for seriously emotionally disturbed students. *Behavioural Disorders, 17*(3), 225–236.

Kallam, M., Hoernicke, P., & Coser, P. (1994). Native Americans and behavior disorders. In R. L. Peterson & S. Ischii-Jordan (Eds.), *Multicultural issues in the education of students with behavioral disorders.* Cambridge, MA: Brookline Books.

Karagiannis, A., Stainback, W., & Stainback, S. (1996). Historical review of inclusion. In S. Stainback & W. Stainback (Eds.), *Inclusion: A guide for educators.* Baltimore, MD: Paul Brookes Publishing.

Kauffman, J. (1997). *Characteristics of emotional and behavioral disorders of children and youth* (6th ed.). Upper Saddle River, NJ: Prentice-Hall Inc.

Kauffman, J. M., & Smucker, K. (1995). The legacies of placement: A brief history of placement options and issues with commentary on their evolution. In J. M. Kauffman, J. W. Lloyd, D. P. Hallahan, & T. A. Astutu (Eds.), *Issues in educational placement: Students with emotional and behavioral disorders* (pp. 21–44). Hillsdale, NJ: Lawrence Erlbaum Associates.

Kelly, K. (1990). Let someone else deal with them: A study of students referred to an activity centre. *set: Research Information for Teachers, 1,* item 4.

King, M. (1993). *Māori: A photographic and social history.* Auckland: Reed Books.

Kounin, J. (1977). *Discipline and group management in classrooms* (Rev. ed.). New York: Holt Rinehart Winston.

Ladson-Billings, G. (1994). What we can learn from multicultural education research. *Education Leadership, 51*(8), 22–26.

Ladson-Billings, G. (1995). Toward a theory of culturally relevant pedagogy. *American Educational Research Journal, 32*(3), 465–491.

Lala, G. (1996). *My life in the gang—the gang in my life: Using self-categorisation theory to understand the role of the gang in former members' lives.* Masters thesis, University of Waikato, New Zealand.

Langley, R. J., Ritchie, J., & Richie, J. (1996). Suicidal behaviour in a bicultural society: A review of gender and cultural differences in adolescents and young persons of Aotearoa New Zealand. *Suicide and Life-threatening Behaviour, 28*(1), 94–106.

Lefrancois, G. (1988). *Psychology for teaching: A bear always faces the front* (6th ed.). Belmont,

CA: Wadsworth Publishing.

Lewis, R. (1997). *The discipline dilemma* (2nd ed.). Melbourne: The Australian Council for Educational Research.

Liberty, K., Clark, B., & Solomon, C. (2000, November–December). *Ecological assessment and children on the borderline*. Paper presented at the annual conference of the New Zealand Association for Research in Education, Hamilton.

Lifelines for students no schools want. *Waikato This Week*. (2000, 13 January). p. 21.

Lipman, P. (1995). Bringing out the best in them: The contribution of culturally relevant teachers to educational reform. *Theory into Practice, 34*(3), 203–208.

Lipsky, D. K., & Gartner, A. (1999). Inclusive education: A requirement of a democratic society. In H. Daniels & P. Garner (Eds.), *World yearbook of education 1999: Inclusive education* (pp. 12–23). London: Kogan Page Limited.

McAllister, G., & Irvine, J. (2002). The role of empathy in teaching culturally diverse students: A qualitative study of teachers' beliefs. *Journal of Teacher Education, 53*(5), 433–443.

McElrea, F. (1994). The intent of the Children, Young Persons' and their Families Act 1989: Restorative justice? *Youth Law Review*, 4–9.

McElrea, F. (1997). *Win-win solutions to school conflict.* A keynote address to the Contemporary Issues in Education Law conference: Strategies for Best Practices, Sydney, Australia.

McInerney, D., & McInerney, V. (1998). *Educationlal psychology: Constructing learning* (2nd ed.). Sydney: Prentice-Hall.

McIntyre, T. (1996). Does the way we teach create behavior disorders in culturally different students. *Education and Treatment of Children, 19*(3), 354–370.

McLeskey, J., & Waldron, N. L. (1998). Responses to questions teachers and administrators frequently ask about inclusive school programmes. *set: Research Information for Teachers, 2*, item 12.

Macfarlane, A. (1995). *Constructing values education programmes in a centre for special learners: A collective responsibility: Me whakaputaina te tūranga, tēnā pea ka tika.* Unpublished MSocSci dissertation, University of Waikato.

Macfarlane, A. (1997). The Hikairo Rationale: Teaching students with emotional and behavioural difficulties: A bicultural approach. *Waikato Journal of Education, 3*, 153–168.

Macfarlane, A. (2000). Listening to culture: Māori principles and practices applied to classroom management. *set: Research Information for teachers, 2*, 23–28.

Macfarlane, A. (2001, August). *Te Hui Whakatika*. Paper presented to the Resource Teachers: Learning and Behaviour (RTLB) Training Programme, Auckland University, Auckland.

Macfarlane, A. (2002). Restorying the individual: The cultural dimension of special education in three Te Arawa sites. *Journal of Māori and Pacific Development 3*(2), 82–89.

Macfarlane, A. (2003). *Culturally inclusive pedagogy for Māori students experiencing learning and behaviour difficulties*. Unpublished doctoral thesis, University of Waikato.

Macfarlane, A. (2004). *Kia hiwa rā! Listen to culture: Māori students' plea to educators*. Wellington: New Zealand Council for Educational Research.

Macfarlane, A. (2005). Inclusion and Māori ecologies: An educultural approach. In D. Fraser, R. Moltzen, & K. Ryba (Eds.), *Learners with special needs in Aotearoa New Zealand* (3rd ed. pp. 99–116). Southbank, Victoria: Thomson/Dunmore Press.

Macfarlane, A. (2006). Becoming educultural: Te Whakawhitinga o ngā mātauranga. Interfacing the knowledge traditions. *Kairāranga Journal of Educational Practice, 7*(2), 41–44.

Macfarlane, A. (2007). In search of a culturally-inclusive curriculum. *Reading Forum NZ, 22*(1), 29–33.

Macfarlane, A., Glynn, T., Cavanagh, T., & Bateman, S. (2005, November). *Creating culturally safe schools: Culturally appropriate approaches to supporting Māori students*. Paper presented at the 7th World Indigenous Peoples Conference on Education (WIPCE), Hamilton, New Zealand.

Macfarlane, A., Glynn, T., Cavanagh, T., & Bateman, S. (2006, September). *Creating culturally safe schools for Māori students*. Paper presented at Te Wehengarua Post Primary Teachers Association (PPTA) Māori Caucus annual conference. Devon Hotel, New Plymouth.

Macfarlane, A., Glynn, T., Grace, W., & Penetito, W. (2005). *He tikanga whakaaro: Mai he tirohanga Māori. A response from a Māori worldview to the proposed New Zealand Curriculum Framework Key Competencies*. A paper prepared for the Ministry of Education. Wellington: Ministry of Education.

Maniapoto, W. (1998). *Cultural assessment training programme*. Seminar to staff, Department of Psychology. Hamilton: University of Waikato.

Marsden, M. (1975). God, man and universe: A Māori worldview. In M. King (Ed.), *Te Ao Hurihuri* (pp. 117–137). Auckland: Reed.

Mead, H. (1997). *A new vision of a better world*. Paper presented at the New Zealand Education Administration Society Conference (NZEAS). In NZEAS Book of Proceedings. Auckland.

Medcalf, J. (1995). Co-operative learning and peer tutoring strategies for inclusive education. *Reading Forum NZ, 2*, 11–19.

Metge, J. (1983). *Learning and teaching: He tikanga Māori*. Wellington: Department of Education.

Meyer, L. H., & Evans, I. M. (2006). *Draft final report: Literature review on intervention with challenging behaviour in children and youth with developmental disabilities*. Wellington: Ministry of Education.

Milligan, A. (2001). Special education policy with regard to adolescents with moderate to severe behaviour needs. *New Zealand Annual Review of Education, 11*, 317–336.

Ministry of Education. (1996). *Special education 2000*. Wellington: Learning Media.

Ministry of Education. (1999). Suspension and expulsion of students from private schools. *Ministry of Education: Education Circular 1999/06.*

Ministry of Education. (2000). *Better relationships for better learning: Guidelines for boards of trustees and schools on engaging with Māori parents, whānau, and communities.* Wellington: Learning Media.

Ministry of Education. (2003). *The Home-School Partnership programme: Literacy focus.* Wellington: Learning Media.

Ministry of Education. (2004). *Attendance, absence and truancy in New Zealand schools in 2004.* A research report. Wellington: Author.

Ministry of Education. (2005). *Report on stand-downs, suspensions, exclusions and expulsions for 2004.* Wellington: Author. Retrieved from (undated), http://www.minedu.govt.nz

Ministry of Education. (2006a). *Educate: Ministry of Education Statement of Intent 2006–2011.* Wellington: Author.

Ministry of Education. (2006b). *Report on secondary teacher workload study.* Wellington: Author.

Mitchell, D. (Ed.). (1999). *Creating inclusive schools.* Hamilton: University of Waikato.

Mitchell, D., Buist, A., Easter, A., Moltzen, R., Macfarlane, A., Quinn, S., & Timutimu, H. (1999). Behavioural strategies. In D. Mitchell (Ed.), *Creating inclusive schools* (p. 33, section 5). Hamilton: University of Waikato.

Mitchell, D., & Mitchell, J. (1985). *Out of the shadows. A chronology of significant events in the development of services for exceptional children and young persons in New Zealand: 1850–1983.* Wellington: Department of Education.

Mitchell, H. A., & Mitchell, M. J. (1998). *Profile of Māori pupils with high marks in School Certificate English and mathematics.* Volume 1: Report. A report prepared for the Department of Education, Wellington.

Moore, D., Anderson, A., & Sharma, U. (2006). *The effectiveness of segregated settings, withdrawal centres, centres of extra support as an intervention for children and young people with severe challenging behaviour.* Final report to New Zealand Ministry of Education. Melbourne: Monash University.

Moore, D., Anderson, A., Timperley, H., Glynn, T., Macfarlane, A., Brown, D., & Thomson, C. (1999). *Caught between stories: Special education in New Zealand.* Wellington: New Zealand Council for Educational Research.

Morris, C. (1996). Contrasting disciplinary models in education. *Thresholds in Education, 22*(4), 7–13.

Morrisey, M. (1997). The uses of culture. *Journal of Intercultural Studies, 18*(2), 93.

Newmann, F. M. (1992). *Student engagement and achievement in American secondary schools.* New York: Teachers College Press.

Noddings, N. (2002). *Educating moral people: An alternative to character education.* New York: Teachers College Press.

O'Connor, M., & Macfarlane, A. H. (2002). New Zealand Māori stories and symbols:

Family value lessons for western counselors. *International Journal for the Advancement of Counselling, 24,* 223–237.

Peer, L., & Reid, G. (2000). *Multilingualism, literacy and dyslexia: A challenge for educators.* London: David Fulton.

Penetito, W. (2004, November). *Theorising a 'place-based education': Ahakoa kai tahi, tērā a roto te hahae ke rā.* Keynote address presented at the annual conference of the New Zealand Association for Research in Education, Wellington.

Penniman, T. (Ed.). (1986). *Makereti: The old-time Māori.* Auckland: New Women's Press.

Pere, R. (1991). *Te Wheke: A celebration of infinite wisdom.* Gisborne: Ao Ako.

Peterson, R., & Ishii-Jordan, S. (Eds.). (1994). *Multicultural issues in the education of students with behavioural disorders.* Cambridge, MA: Brookline Books.

Phinney J., & Rotheram, M. (1987). *Children's ethnic socialization: Pluralism and development.* Newbury Park: Sage Publications.

Pierce, C. (1996). The importance of classroom climate for at-risk learners. In *set special 1996: Students at risk,* item 10. Wellington: New Zealand Council for Educational Research; Melbourne: Australian Council for Educational Research.

Porter, L. (1996). *Student behaviour: Theory and practice for teachers.* St Leonards, NSW: Allen & Unwin.

Porter, L. (2000). *Behaviour in schools: Theory and practice for teachers.* Buckingham, UK: Open University Press.

Preedy, M. (1989). *Approaches to curriculum management.* Philadelphia: Open University Press.

Prochnow, J. E., Kearney, A. C., & Carroll-Lind, J. (2000). Successful inclusion: What do teachers say they need? *New Zealand Journal of Educational Studies, 35* (2), 157–177.

Ramsay, P., Hawk, K., Harold, B., Marriott, R., & Poskitt, J. (1993). *Developing partnerships. Collaboration between teachers and parents.* Wellington: Learning Media.

Reedy, T. (1992). *Barriers and constraints that affect Māori educational outcomes.* Wellington: Reedy Holdings.

Reinke, W., & Herman, K. (2002). Creating school environments that deter antisocial behaviours in youth. *Psychology in the schools, 39*(5), 549–559.

Rietveld, C. (1999). Just leave him out! Inclusion in the junior classroom: What is involved? In *set special 1999: Special education,* item 1. Wellington: New Zealand Council for Educational Research; Melbourne: Australian Council for Educational Research.

Ritchie, J. (1992). *Becoming bicultural.* Wellington: Huia Publishers.

Robinson, T., & Howard-Hamilton, M. (2000). *The convergence of race, ethnicity, and gender: Multiple identities in counselling.* Upper Saddle River, NJ: Prentice-Hall.

Rogers, W. (1990). *You know the fair rule: Strategies for making the hard job of discipline in school easier*. Hawthorn, Victoria: Australian Council for Educational Research.

Rogers, W. (1995). *A whole-school approach to behaviour management*. Gosford, NSW: Scholastic Pty Limited.

Rogers, W. (1997). *Cracking the hard class: Strategies for managing the harder than average class*. Sydney: Scholastic Australia.

Rogoff, B. (2003). *The cultural nature of human development*. New York: Oxford University Press.

Rutter, M., Maugham, B., Mortimer, P., & Ouston, J. (1979). *Fifteen thousand hours: Secondary schools and their effects on children*. London: Open Books.

Ryan, R., & Stiller, J. (1991). The social contexts of internalisation: Parent influences on autonomy, motivation and achievement. In M. I. Maher & P. I. Pintrich, *Advances in motivation and achievement* (pp.115–149). Greenwich: JAI Press.

Senge, P., Cambron-McCabe, N., Lucas, T., Smith, B., Dutton, J., & Kleiner, A. (2000). *Schools that learn: A fifth discipline fieldbook for educators, parents, and everyone who cares about education*. London: Nicholas Brealey.

Sergiovanni, T. (1994). *Building community in schools*. San Francisco: Jossey-Bass.

Sharpe, S. (1998). How much does bullying hurt? The effects of bullying on the health, happiness and educational progress of secondary aged students. *Educational and Child Psychology, 12*, 81–88.

Shea, T. M., & Bauer, A. M. (1991). *Parents and teachers of children with exceptionalities*. Boston: Allyn & Bacon.

Silva, P., & Stanton, W. (Eds.). (1996). *From child to adult: The Dunedin multidisciplinary health and development study*. Auckland: Oxford University Press.

Simon, J. (1993). *Provision for Māori in state secondary schools: An ethnographic study*. Auckland: Research Unit for Māori Education, University of Auckland.

Simpson, R. (1996). *Working with parents and families of exceptional children and youth: Techniques for successful conferencing and collaboration* (3rd ed.). Austin, TX: Pro-Ed.

Skinner, B. F. (1971). *Beyond freedom and dignity*. New York: Knopf Publishing.

Slavin, R. (1990). *Cooperative learning: Theory, research and practice*. Englewood Cliffs, NJ: Prentice Hall.

Smith, C., & Laslett, R. (1993). *Effective classroom management: A teacher's guide* (2nd ed.). London: Routledge.

Smith, G. (1995). Whakaoho whānau: New formations of whānau as an innovative intervention into Māori cultural and educational crises. *He Pukenga Kōrero, 1* (1), 18–36.

Smith, R. (2002). *Creating the effective primary school: A guide for school leaders and teachers*. London: Stylus Publishing.

Smith, T., Polloway, E., Patton, J., & Dowdy, C. (2004). *Teaching students with special needs in inclusive settings* (4th ed.). Boston: Allyn & Bacon.

Smith, P., & Morita, Y. (1999). Introduction. In P. Smith, Y. Morita, J. Junger-Tas, D.

Olweus, R. Catalano, & P. Slee, *The Nature of bullying* (pp. 1–4). London: Routledge.

Spoonley, P. (1988). *Racism and ethnicity.* Auckland: Oxford University Press.

Stafford, D. (1967). *Te Arawa: A history of the Arawa people.* Wellington; Auckland: Reed Publishing.

Stainback, S., & Stainback, W., East, K., & Sapon-Shevin, M. (1994). A commentary on inclusion and the development of a positive self-identity by people with disabilities. *Exceptional Children, 60,* 486–490.

Stanford, G. (1997). *Successful urban African-American teachers.* Pennsylvania: University of Delaware.

Stanley, P. (2006, September). *Risk and resilience.* Presentation to a postgraduate class at the University of Waikato, Hamilton.

Stanovich, P., & Jordan, A. (1998). Canadian teachers' and principals' beliefs about inclusive education as predictors of effective teaching in heterogeneous classrooms. *The Elementary School Journal, 98*(3), 221–238.

Sugai, G. (2003). Commentary: Establishing efficient and durable systems of school based support. *School Psychology Review,* 2003, *12*(4), 530–535.

Sugai, G. (2004, September). *School-wide positive behaviour support: Defining features and outcomes.* Keynote address presented to the Australian Association of Special Education, Hobart.

Tate, H. (1990). The unseen world. *New Zealand Geographic, 5,* 87–92.

Thomas, G., & Loxley, A. (2001). *Deconstructing special education and constructing inclusion.* Buckingham, UK: Open University Press.

Trevett, C. (2006, 27 September). Remove violent pupils—principal. *The New Zealand Herald,* p. 1.

Vercoe, A. (1998). *Educating Jake: Pathways to empowerment.* Auckland: HarperCollins.

Villegas, A., & Lucas, T. (2002). *Educating culturally responsive teachers: A coherent approach.* Albany: State University of New York Press.

Vygotsky, L. (1978). *Mind and society.* Cambridge, MA: Harvard University Press.

Walker, J., & Shea, T. (1999). *Behaviour management: A practical approach for educators* (7th ed.). Upper Saddle River, NJ: Prentice-Hall.

Walker, R. (1991). *Liberating Māori from educational subjugation.* Auckland: Research Unit for Māori Education, University of Auckland.

Watson, A. J., & Giorcelli, L. R. (1999). *Accepting the literacy challenge.* Gosford, NSW: Scholastic Australia.

Wearmouth, J., Glynn, T., & Berryman, M. (2005). *Perspectives on student behaviour in schools: Exploring theory and developing practice.* London: Routledge.

Wheldall, K. (1992). *Discipline in schools: Psychological perspectives on the Elton Report.* New York: Routledge.

Wheldall, K., & Merrett, F. (1989). Managing troublesome behaviour in primary and secondary classrooms. *The Best of set: Discipline,* item 12. Wellington: New Zealand Council for Educational Research; Melbourne: Australian Council for Educational Research.

Williams, H. (1971). *A dictionary of the Māori language* (7th ed.). Wellington: Government Printer.

Wilton, K. (1997, April). *Special education policy for children with moderate learning or behavioural difficulties in New Zealand: Does "inclusion" really mean "exclusion"?* Lecture presented at the national conference of the New Zealand Special Education Association, Auckland.

Winzer, M., & Mazurek, K. (1998). *Special education in multicultural contexts.* Upper Saddle River, NJ: Prentice-Hall.

Wright, D. (1998). *Managing behaviour in the classroom.* Melbourne: Heinemann.

Wylie, C. (2006, April). *Why key competencies matter.* Keynote address, New Zealand Council for Educational Research conference, Wellington.

Ysseldyke, J., & Christensen, S. (1998). *TIES II: The instructional environmental system – II* (4th ed.). Longmont, CO: Sopris West.

Glossary of Māori terms

āhua—attitude, demeanour

aroha—love, acceptance, inclusion

ata mārie—salutation, morning greeting

haka—combination of verse and expressive movement

hapū—clan, subtribe

Hei Awhina Maatua programme—education and health programme designed for helping parents and children

Hikairo—illustrious ancestor of the Te Arawa people

Hikairo Rationale—An educational intervention approach based on a blend of assertiveness and warmth

hinengaro—mind, relating to the cognitive dimension

hui—literally a meeting, a gathering wherein certain rituals apply

Hui Whakatika—Restorative Conference, an approach that draws from traditional Māori discipline

iwi—tribe

kaiako—teacher

kaiārahi—leader, adviser

kaiawhina—teacher assistant, teacher aide

kai—food, refreshments, nourishment

kaikōrero—orator, speaker

kaitiaki—classroom assistant
kānohi ki te kānohi—face-to-face interchanges
kapa haka—performing arts group
karakia—prayer, incantation
kaumātua—respected older person(s)
kaupapa Māori—Māori philosophy
kaupapa—philosophy, theme, content
kawa—protocol
kia mau—a statement for paying attention
kia ora—salutation, common expression for greeting and acknowledging
Kīngitanga—the King movement, New Zealand Māori monarchy
kōhanga reo—language nest, preschool teaching through the medium of Māori
kōrero—discussion, talk
koro—respected older Māori man
kōtahitanga—unity, togetherness, bonding
kuia—respected older Māori woman
kura kaupapa Māori—primary school, teaching throgh the medium of Māori
kura—school
Maatua Whāngai—Māori Service Provider, located in most parts of New Zealand
manaakitanga—the ethic of caring and hospitality
mana—status, identity, dignity, authority, integrity
manuhiri—visitor(s)
Māori Wardens Association—New Zealand wide organisation, provides community-based services
Māori—indigenous people of Aotearoa, New Zealand
Māoritanga—the way of life, the principles of living that encapsulates "being Māori"
marae—community meeting place
matua—senior man, male teacher
mau-rākau—long-staff weaponry drills
mihi whakamutanga—closing remarks, usually made at a meeting
mihimihi—the process of acknowledgement by one to others
Mokoia Wānanga—place of higher learning, domiciled on an island named Mokoia
orangatanga—a state of being nurtured
poukai—annual pilgrimage carried out by the New Zealand Māori monarchy
Princess Te Puea—revered ancestor and chieftainess of the Waikato people
rākau—tree
rangatahi—youth

raupatu—land confiscations

rohe—district

taha Māori—Māori aspects

taiaha—long staff

tamariki—children

Tāne Mahuta—the progenitor of forests, plants, and humankind

tangata whenua—people of the land, indigenous people

te ao Māori—Māori view of the world including philosophies and values systems

Te Arawa— ancestral canoe and tribe in Bay of Plenty

Te Kooti—illustrious ancestor warrior, powerful personality of the Rongowhakaata tribe

Te Marautanga o Aotearoa—the curriculum for kura kaupapa Māori

Te Rākau—The metaphor of "The Tree" as a symbol for wholesome progress

te reo Māori me ōna tikanga—Māori language and customs

te reo Māori—the Māori language

Te Rerenga ā te Pīrere—literally means The Flight of the Fledgling; the title given to a longitudinal study of 111 Kohanga reo and kura kaupapa Māori students

Te Wheke—The octopus; metaphor portraying key concepts for enhancing health and education

Te wiki o te reo Māori— Māori language week, a time when Māori language is advocated across New Zealand schools, and other entities

tikanga—customary aspects of Māori culture, customs

tinana—body, relating to physical dimensions of person

tipuna—ancestors

tuakana—older person, in this case a more senior student

tukutuku—ornamental lattice work

tumeke—colloquialism meaning "terrific"

Tū tangata—community support programme

tumuaki—principal

wairua—spirit, spiritual, underpinning feeling(s)

waiata—song

wānanga—place of higher learning

whāea—senior woman, female teacher

whaikōrero—oratory

whakataukī—proverb

whakawhanungatanga—building relationships

whānau—the extended family

whanaungatanga—relationships

Index

abuse 36, 67
academic skills, attainment of 74–75, 77, 79, 80, 102, 103, 110
accountability of teachers 100, 101, 102
Achievement in Multicultural High Schools project (AIMHI) 107–112, 134
active listening 137
African-American teachers and students 98, 99–105, 110
aggression 18, 23, 41, 45, 55, 71, 73, 81, 93, 157
    nonphysical 84
    verbal 82, 116, 122, 125, 154
āhua 129
ako 136, 141
alienation 16
alternative education programmes 76–77, 151
anxiety 64, 65, 67–68, 83
apathy 80
aptitude 31
aroha 42, 118, 128, 129, 157
assertiveness 127–133, 162
    Māori models of 128
at-risk students 71–72, 76, 77, 92, 103, 104

definition 152
attachment
    response by teachers 21
    students, to school 163
attending to students 137
authoritarianism 127, 128, 129
authority, personal 128, 132
avoidance 64, 65, 66–67
Awhinatia: toward restorative practice 151–161

Bateman, Sonja 85
behaviour continuum 45–46
behaviour difficulties
    antecedents 60
    chronicity 44
    definitions 42–44
    frequency 44
    historical 15–16
    severity 44
    types 44–46
    See also serious behaviour difficulties; severe behaviour difficulties; and specific types of behaviour difficulties
behaviour management programmes, whole-school 171–174

behaviour modification 29, 30
behavioural model 29–30, 43
belief, student 163
Berryman, Mere 56
biculturalism 76–77, 116, 143, 145
biophysical model 28–29, 43
body language 57, 58–59, 104, 109, 138
Bower's definition of severe behaviour disorders 43, 47
bullying 67, 68, 71, 82, 83–84, 154
  NO-BLAME approach to 85–88

Canter, Lee and Marlene 56, 127
care, context of 100, 103, 107, 135–136, 137
categorisation 16, 17
Centres for Extra Support (CES) 19
circumspection 16, 17
"city arabs" 15
classroom
  as community 100, 102
  learning environment 53–54, 102, 104–105
  "safe-haven" status 104–105, 109, 127, 133, 135, 136
classroom management 31, 51–70, 92, 105
  chores 58
  landmark studies 55–59
  meetings 60
  "noise level register" 61, 74
  room arrangement 58, 59, 141
  rules 58, 123–124
  Smith and Laslett's rules 52–53, 111
  See also discipline
"collaborative storying" 106
collective responsibility (student, whānau, school) 74
commitment, student 163
communication 52, 59, 70, 110
  intercultural 133–134
  nonverbal 57, 58–59, 104, 109, 138
  polarised 119
  with parents/caregivers 63
community
  as learning environment 53
  classroom 100, 102
  Māori, significance of involvement 144

community identity, teacher 101, 111, 148
community networks, school 148
concern, response by teachers 22
conferences, restorative 152–161
consensus 151, 153, 172
constructivist approaches 136
control procedures 27, 30
Cookson-Cox, Candy 88–89
co-operative learning 140–142
counselling 27, 81
crime, juvenile 15, 41
cultural competence 98
cultural connectedness 103, 126
cultural identity 42, 99, 103, 116
cultural influences on behaviour 33, 38–40, 54
culturally relevant pedagogy 99
culturally responsive teaching 33, 39, 40, 54, 58, 97–113, 134–135
  Achievement in Multicultural High Schools project (AIMHI) 107–112, 134
  and student conferences 153
  Cecelia Pierce study 104–105
  characteristics of exceptional teachers 110
  Gloria Ladson-Billings study 99–100
  Grace Stanford study 100–102
  Hei Awhina Maatua programme 134
  Pauline Lipman study 103
  Te Kōtahitanga 105–107, 134
  See also Hikairo Rationale
culture, definition 39

DARE Foundation Skills for Life programmes 92
decile ranking of schools 19
  decile 1 category 107
defiance 45, 46, 58, 64, 65–66, 73, 82, 93
deficit theories 28
Department of Education Activity Centre 73
depression 43, 47
developmental theories 28
discipline 51–52, 55–56, 60–69. See also classroom management
  Jones model 57–59
  options of last resort 90–91

discrimination 30
dishonesty 18
disobedience 55, 116
disruptive behaviour 45, 46, 52, 54, 64
   in the hallway 69
   profile of students most likely to be involved 71–72
   teachers' control strategies for 56–57
   to prevent behaviour difficulties 59
District Truancy Services 90
drug/substance abuse 71, 73, 116, 152
Dunedin longitudinal study 36

easy change 90, 91
ecological model 31, 43
ecological paradigm 20, 21, 24
Education Act 1999 88
Education and Science Committee Inquiry into Children at Risk Through Truancy and Behavioural Problems 36
Education Support Personnel (ESP) 92
educational approaches, evolution of 16–17
Effective Teaching Profile, Te Kōtahitanga 107
emotional factors in nonengagement 65, 67–68
empathy 136, 137
ethnic harassment 84
environment. *See* influencing environments; learning environment
evidence-based practice 34
examination, in school conferences 153
exclusion 91
exclusionary time-out 90
expulsion 45, 91, 151, 160
externalised behaviours 18
extinction 30
eye contact 58, 138

facial expression 59
fairness contract 125, 130–131
family group conferences 160, 161
family influences on behaviour 16, 31, 36–37, 41, 72, 104
   at-risk families, types 37
   truancy 89

   See also home and school, linking; parents/caregivers; whānau
forgotten materials or work, by students 63–64
functional limitations paradigm 20, 21

gangs 41–43, 124, 130
generalisation 30
genetic disorders 28
Ginott, Haim 56
Glasser, William 56
Glynn, Ted 56
Golden Apple Foundation, Chicago 100–101
goofing off 45
Grossman, Herbert 56
"group alerting" 57
Group Special Education (GSE) 19, 90, 149, 161

hā 163
hapū 32, 120, 151
Hei Awhina Maatua programme 134
Hikairo Rationale 73, 115–165
   awhinatia: toward restorative practice 151–161
   designing 116–119
   huakina mai: opening doorways 119–127
   i runga i te manaaki 133–138
   ihi: being assertive 127–133
   kōtahitanga: linking home and school 143–151
   orangatanga: developing a nurturing environment 162–163
   rangatiratanga: motivating learners 138–143
"hindering other children" 54
hinengaro 153
holistic teaching 100, 101, 102, 136
holistic world view 163–164
home and school, linking 143–151
   home school contact book 63
home environment. *See* family influences on behaviour; parents/caregivers; whānau
Home-School Partnership Training Programme 150

huakina mai: opening doorways
    119–127
"human connection" 75
Hui Whakatika 153–161
    sequence of steps for 156-157
humour 109, 137
hyperactivity 81

i runga i te manaaki 133–138
identity
    community 101
    cultural 42, 99, 103, 116
    family and personal 41, 42
ihi: being assertive 127–133
immorality 45
inattention 45
inclusion 16, 17–18, 20, 68, 151
    and behaviour difficulties 18–19, 20,
    24, 80, 94
    teachers' perceptions of 21–23, 24
inclusionary time-out 90–91
indifference, response by teachers 22
influencing environments 31, 35–47. *See
    also* cultural influences on behaviour;
    family influences on behaviour;
    learning environment; peer influences
    on behaviour; school influences
    on behaviour; home environment;
    television
institutionalisation 16, 17
instruction 31, 52, 132
integration 16, 17
internalised behaviours 18
interventions 27, 28, 31, 54–55
    early intervention 36
    landmark studies 55–59
    mild/moderate behaviour difficulties
    60–69
    severe behaviour difficulties 71–94
    See also specific interventions
intimidation 55, 67, 154
involvement, student 163
isolation 16, 17
iwi 32, 120, 121, 148, 151

Jones, Fredric 55, 56, 57–59

kaikōrero 128
"kānohi ki te kānohi" 141–142

kapahaka 141, 148
karakia 156, 157, 159
kaumātua 128, 148, 155, 159, 160
kaupapa Māori theory 159
    research principles 106
    whānau as core feature of 75
Kia Hiwa Ra! Listen to Culture 138–139
Kia Kaha 92
kōhanga reo 135, 148
kōtahitanga 76, 143, 150
Kōtahitanga: linking home and school
    143–151
Kounin, Jacob 55–57
kura kaupapa Māori 135

labelling 16, 28, 120–121
Ladson-Billings, Gloria 99–100
laissez-faire families 37
Lala, Girish 41–42
learning
    co-operative 140–142
    self-regulated 139, 140
learning environment 53–54, 80, 102,
    104–105. *See also* academic skills,
    attainment of
    effective 174–175
    nurturing 102, 162–163
lesson content 53
lesson control 55–57
life-space interviewing 27, 81, 82
Lipman, Pauline 103
listening, active 137

Maatua Whāngai 148
mainstreaming 16, 17. *See also* inclusion
Makereti 32
mana 40, 53, 80, 128, 138, 150, 155, 160,
    165
mana tangata 138
mana whenua 138
manaakitanga 74, 76, 111, 112, 119, 128,
    133–138, 157
managerial function of teachers 52,
    132–133
Māori
    cultural identity 42
    cultural values 40, 74, 76
    gangs 41–42

learning activities and routines 74, 76–77
models of assertiveness 128
parents 121–123, 144, 146–148, 159
social ecology 32
students 19, 72, 73, 74, 98, 105–107, 110, 111, 117, 126, 134–135, 139–140
See also Hikairo Rationale; Te Kōtahitanga; whānau
Māori Wardens Association 148
marae 76, 121, 122, 128, 133, 148
visits to 76
mauri 163
medical treatment 28–29
medication, administering 29
mentoring 122, 125
mihimihi 157
morning 129–130
mini time-out 90–91
Ministry of Education 73, 89–90, 91, 92, 105, 108, 116, 117, 147–148, 150, 151–152
Group Special Education (GSE) 19, 90, 149, 161
Restorative Conferencing in Schools Trial 152
School Support Services 150
Suspension Reduction Initiative (SRI) 151, 152
Ministry of Māori Development 76
Mokoia Island 118
wānanga 125–126, 135
motivation, student 52, 58, 80, 108, 109, 136, 138–143

negative reinforcement 30, 55, 64
New Zealand Police 85, 92
Ngāti Rangiwewehi 117–118, 125–126
NO-BLAME approach to bullying 85–88
"noise level register", classroom 61, 74
noncompliance 18
nonengagement in class work or activities 64–65
nonverbal communication 57, 58–59, 104, 109, 138
norms and values 76, 103, 115

openmindness 137
orangatanga 119, 162–163

Papakura, Maggie 32
parental discord and divorce 36, 72
parents/caregivers 63, 104, 121, 152
Māori 121–123, 139, 144, 146–148, 159
Pasifika 150
significance of involvement 144
See also family influences on behaviour; home and school, linking; whānau
participation 20
Pasifika parents 150
Pasifika students 98, 107, 110, 111
passivity 127
patience 137
peer influences on behaviour 31, 38, 40–42, 140, 152
Māori students 106
truancy 89
Pierce, Cecelia 104–105
polarised communication 119
pono 157
positive reinforcement 27, 30, 55, 63
Poutama Pounamu Research Centre 134
poverty 36, 152
prevention of unacceptable behaviour 58, 59–60, 61, 63
professional assistance for teachers 149–151
professional development 112
bicultural 145–146
proximity control 59, 65, 66, 82, 138
psychodynamic model 26–28, 43, 81
psychotherapy 27
punishment 55
put-downs 82–83
low-level verbal 68–69

Railway School 72–81
cultural presence 76
hidden curriculum 75–76
linking practice and theory 80
regular curriculum 74–75
staff-related issues 79–81
student comments 77–79
rangatiratanga: motivating learners 138–143
reality-therapy interviewing 27
reciprocity 101, 108, 109, 125, 133, 134, 141, 163

reconciliation 153
Redl, Fritz 55, 56
reinforcement 55, 90, 111, 124–125. *See also* negative reinforcement; positive reinforcement
rejection, response by teachers 22
resilience 139
Resource Teachers Learning and Behaviour (RTLB) service 19, 149–150, 161
respect 101, 107, 108, 109, 115, 121, 124, 125, 133, 162, 170
   and conferencing 159
   between teachers, professionals and parents/ whānau 146–146
restoration 153
Restorative Conferencing in Schools Trial 152
restorative practice 151–161
restricted families 37
Richmond School 171–172
"ripple effect" 57
Rodney District Council Truancy Action Group 88

"safe-haven", classroom 104–105, 109, 127, 133, 135, 136
scaffolded tutoring 136
segregation 16, 20
self control
   student 91
   teacher 58
self-efficacy, student 67
self-esteem, student 67, 73, 80, 121, 127, 140, 142, 147
self-regulated learners 139, 140
serious behaviour difficulties 46
severe behaviour difficulties 43, 44, 45, 46
   options of last resort 90–91
   Railway School case study 71–81
   responses to specific difficulties 81–90
   special programmes for 92
sexual harassment 84
school
   and truancy 89
   collective responsibility, with whānau and student 74

influences on behaviour 31, 37–38
learning environment 53
whole-school behaviour-management programmes 171–174
shaping 27, 30
Skinner, B.F. 56
social factors in nonengagement 65, 67–68
socialisation 32, 36, 37, 141
sociocultural model 32–33, 43
special education
   developments in New Zealand 18–20
   Moderate Behaviour Initiative 19
   Severe Behaviour Initiative 19–20
Special Education 2000 (SE2000) policy 18–19, 23
Special Education Grant (SEG) 19
special programmes 92
stand-down 91, 116–117, 122, 151
Stanford, Grace 100–102
stigmatisation 16, 17
Student Engagement Initiative 90
substance abuse 71, 73, 116, 152
suspension 45, 91, 103, 116–117, 151
Suspension Reduction Initiative (SRI) 151, 152
swearing
   high-level 81–82
   low–level 64

tagging 71
Tainui 149
talking by students, at inappropriate times 54, 61
tangata whenua 120
Te Arawa 126, 135
Te Kōtahitanga 105–107, 134
Te Rākau 119, 162, 165
Te Rerenga ā te Pīrere 135
Te Wheke model 164
teacher-student interactions/relationships 38, 39, 52, 53, 54, 70, 80, 101–102, 103
   Achievement in Multicultural High Schools project 108–109, 110–112
   Hikairo Rationale 115, 120–121, 123–125, 127, 128, 129–132, 136–137
   Te Kōtahitanga 106, 107
   See also culturally-responsive teaching

teachers
    accountability 100, 101, 102
    African-American 98, 99–105
    and truancy 89
    artistes 97, 98
    as role models 76, 105, 109, 140, 162
    authoritarian 127, 128, 129
    calmness 58, 66
    competence 20
    confidence 20, 59, 108
    control strategies 55–57
    effective, characteristics of 79, 107, 113, 174–175
    empathetic 136, 137
    enthusiastic 105, 112, 139
    heroic and valiant 97, 98, 110–112
    instructional function 52, 132
    managerial function 52, 132–133
    perceptions of inclusion 21–23, 24
    permissive 127
    professional assistance for 149–151
    professional development 112, 145–146, 175
    roles 16, 105
    self-control 58
    stress, sources of 170
    support for 20, 22–23, 24, 29, 174
    threats to 71, 93
    workload 169–170, 172
    See also classroom management; culturally-responsive teaching; interventions
television 31
theoretical models 25–26, 33–34, 43
    behavioural 29–30, 43
    biophysical 28–29, 43
    ecological 31, 43
    psychodynamic 26–28, 43
    sociocultural 32–33, 43
tika 157
tikanga Māori 135, 159
time-out 90–91
tinana 153
token economy 30
truancy 73, 88–90, 147, 154
Tū Tangata programme 92
tuakana 122, 125, 141
tuakana-teina 136

unhappiness 47
United States 98, 99–100, 116, 136
unrest, student
    at beginning of activity 62–63
    on entering classroom 61–62
unsafe families 37

vandalism 71
verbal abuse 82, 116, 122, 125, 154
violence 15, 46, 116
Vygotsky, L. 32, 140, 142

waiata 157
wairua 75, 153, 160
wānanga 125–126, 135, 148
Wattenberg, William 55, 56
Wearmouth, Janice 56
whakamā 40, 80
whānau 32, 36, 74, 79, 122, 123, 135
    and Hui Whakatika 154, 155, 160, 161
    and Kia Kaha 92
    collective responsibility, with student and school 74
    core feature of kaupapa Māori theory 75
    in Whare Tapa Whā model 164
    relationship of teachers and professionals with 146–148
    significance of involvement 144
    See also family influences on behaviour; home and school, linking; parents/caregivers
whanaungatanga 74, 160
Whare Tapa Whā model 164
whole-school behaviour management programmes 171–174
withdrawal 21, 23, 81, 83
    short-term 23
"withitness" 128, 138

Youth Education Service (YES) 92

zone of proximal development 32, 140, 142

ALSO AVAILABLE FROM NZCER

Kia hiwa ra! Listen to culture
—Māori students' plea to educators

Angus H Macfarlane

"Kia hiwa ra" literally means "to be alert". This book is intended to alert teachers to models of good teaching in diverse classrooms and to encourage them to be alert to the various cultures that are represented. If we want to extend academic achievement for Māori students, we need to create a strong foundation for their learning. This foundation includes building upon students' cultural and experiential strengths to help them acquire new skills and knowledge.

This book records the work and thoughts of culturally relevant teachers, all of whom demonstrate connectedness with students and who see their classrooms as places where they "listen to culture" in order to forge meaningful relationships that enhance the quality of the learning environment.

Kia Hiwa Ra is a book which can help all teachers to become "educultural": helping them to understand themselves, their culture, and the culture of others—and to be more successful with all students.

NZCER 2004   ISBN 1-877293-29-6   RRP: $24.75

ORDER FROM

NZCER Sales, PO Box 3237, Wellington
Phone: 04 802 1450   Fax: 04 384 7933
Email: sales@nzcer.org.nz

A full list of NZCER publications is available on the Internet.
Check out our site at www.nzcer.org.nz

The Cultural Self-Review:
Providing culturally effective, inclusive education for Māori learners

Jill Bevan-Brown

The Cultural Self-Review provides a structure and process that teachers from early childhood centres through to secondary schools can use to explore how well they cater for Māori learners, including those with special needs. It is a user-friendly resource that enables strengths to be celebrated and built on, weaknesses to be identified and worked on, and communication between teachers, parents, whānau, and the Māori community to be promoted for the ultimate benefit of everyone concerned.

Central to the book is a cultural input framework which provides a set of principles for analysing programme components including: environment, personnel, policy, processes, content, resources, assessment, and administration. While there is an emphasis on practical ideas in this guide for conducting a cultural self-review, a recipe-book approach is not recommended. Schools and early childhood services will be able to use the ideas as a springboard for discussion and for developing strategies that meet their particular needs and which are appropriate for their unique circumstances.

NZCER 2003   ISBN 1-877293-25-3   RRP: $27.00

ORDER FROM

NZCER Sales, PO Box 3237, Wellington
Phone: 04 802 1450   Fax: 04 384 7933
Email: sales@nzcer.org.nz

A full list of NZCER publications is available on the Internet.
Check out our site at www.nzcer.org.nz

Māori Parents and Education
Ko Ngā Mātua Māori me te Mātauranga

Sheridan McKinley with Anne Else

This book presents the perspectives of Māori parents as they talk about education and their aspirations for, and their concerns about, their children's schooling. It provides valuable insights which may contribute to shaping better home-school relationships for Māori parents and children.

The parents in the study wanted their children to have a better education than they had, and expressed a strong wish to be involved in their child's schooling. The key factor is school outreach. When teachers reach out into the community, showing their respect for the relationships and activities which matter for Māori parents and their children, partnership with parents appears to be more readily achieved. How well Māori children do at school is strongly linked with how well parents and children relate to school staff.

This book is an abridged version of the major research report Māori Parents and Education: Ko Ngā Mātua Māori me te Mātauranga.

NZCER 2002   ISBN 1-877293-13-X   RRP: $19.80

ORDER FROM

NZCER Sales, PO Box 3237, Wellington
Phone: 04 802 1450   Fax: 04 384 7933
Email: sales@nzcer.org.nz

A full list of NZCER publications is available on the Internet.
Check out our site at www.nzcer.org.nz